THE AMERICAN GARDEN ASSOCIATION

ANNUALS
GARDEN GUIDES

THE AMERICAN GARDEN ASSOCIATION

ANNUALS

GARDEN GUIDES

DEREK FELL

SMITHMARK

A FRIEDMAN GROUP BOOK

This edition published in 1992 by SMITHMARK Publishers Inc.,
16 East 32nd Street, New York, NY 10016.

ISBN 0-8317-6936-X

THE AMERICAN GARDEN ASSOCIATION GARDEN GUIDES: ANNUALS
was prepared and produced by
Michael Friedman Publishing Group, Inc.
15 West 26th Street
New York, NY 10010

Editor: Dana Rosen
Art Director: Jeff Batzli
Designer: Tanya Ross-Hughes
Photography Editor: Christopher C. Bain
Production: Jeanne Kaufman

Typeset by Bookworks Plus
Color separations by Bright Arts Pte. Ltd.
Printed and bound in Hong Kong by Leefung-Asco Printers Ltd.

Acknowledgments

The author wishes to thank Peggy Fisher for help with research, Kathy Nelson for help with typing the manuscript, Wendy Fields for help with picture selections, and Carolyn Heath for help with styling some of the floral compositions.

CONTENTS

ANNUALS: INSTANT COLOR

WHAT IS AN ANNUAL?

Strictly speaking, an annual is any plant that completes its life cycle in a year. The life cycle includes germinating from seed, sprouting leaves, producing flowers, developing seed pods, scattering seeds for a new generation of plants, and finally dying—either from frost or from sheer exhaustion.

To capitalize on the public's desire for instant gratification, seed companies occasionally classify certain biennials and perennials as annuals because, like annuals, they flower the first year. Foxgloves, for example, are biennials; they complete their life cycle in two years, growing a crown of leaves the first year and flowering the second. But the variety 'Foxy', if started early from seed sown indoors and transplanted to the garden, will flower the first year. The hardy hibiscus (*Hibiscus moscheutos*) is normally a perennial; it grows a clump of leaves the first year, flowers the second year, and then flowers year after year. However, the variety 'Southern Belle' is a hybrid that will flower the first year like an annual if seed is started early indoors, and then it will continue to flower in subsequent years as a perennial.

Annuals are classified as "hardy" (tolerates hard frosts) and "tender" (killed by frost). You sometimes see the term "half-hardy annual"; this means the plant will tolerate mild frosts.

Annuals are also classified as "cool season" (these are usually hardy annuals), flowering best during cool conditions in spring and autumn; and "warm season" (these are usually tender annuals), flowering best during hot, sunny summers.

What annuals provide more than any other plant category is instant color. Some annuals—such as alyssum, marigolds, and zinnias—will bloom within five weeks from seed, allowing them to be transplanted to the garden in full bloom.

Annuals also provide intense color. Portulaca, petunias, and celosia, for example, have lots of shimmering flowers that reflect the sun. Sometimes the flowering display is so dramatic, the blossoms seem to completely hide the foliage.

Many annuals are "continuous flowering." Once they start to bloom, they don't stop until killed by frost or until they drop from the exhaustion of setting seeds. Because of their ability to bloom over an entire season, annuals are frequently used to embellish other plantings that are more short-lived in their flowering, such as perennial beds and shrub borders.

You can add annuals to your garden in two ways: by planting seed or by using transplants. Seeds can be purchased at local garden centers or from mail-order houses, which generally offer a larger selection. Transplants are generally purchased from garden centers. Certain important considerations will influence which method you decide to choose.

BOTANICAL NOMENCLATURE

The plant kingdom is composed of families. One of the largest among annuals is the Compositae family, commonly called the daisy family because most of its members (called genera, singular: genus) have flowers with a button center surrounded by a single layer of slender, pointed petals typical of daisies.

Three familiar genera in the daisy family are sunflowers (*Helianthus*), mums (*Chrysanthemum*), and marigolds (*Tagetes*). Within each genus are species—usually wild plants with distinctive characteristics. For example, *Tagetes patula* is a dwarf, compact, small-flowered marigold native to Mexico, but it is commonly called the French marigold because it first became popular as a garden plant in France. It has multiple layers of petals that create a ball shape. This characteristic is called "double-flowered."

Another wild species of *Tagetes* is *tenuifolia*, commonly called the signet marigold because at one time its botanical name was *Tagetes signata*. These marigolds are dwarf and compact like the French, but they are single-flowered and smaller, creating a cushionlike habit.

Sometimes plant breeders develop special forms either by selection within one species or by hybridizing (crossing two or more species). Selections usually have variety names to identify them. For example, *Tagetes patula* 'Petite' describes a special dwarf selection of the French marigold. Hybrids can also have variety names, but to indicate a hybrid the symbol " × " is used. For example, *Tagetes × hybrida* 'Triploid' identifies a group of hybrids developed from crossing the tall *Tagetes erecta* with the dwarf *Tagetes patula* to create an incredibly vigorous, free-flowering series.

SEED STARTING

Some annuals are best direct-seeded and others should be started indoors. Shirley poppies, for example, should be direct-seeded. They resent any kind of root disturbance and perform best when the seed is lightly scattered over the soil surface and covered with just enough soil to anchor it. To ensure rapid germination from direct-seeding, be sure the soil surface is kept moist, and don't sow tender annuals like zinnias until danger of frost has passed. Some thinning may be necessary to give direct-seeded plants room to grow.

Annuals may need to be started indoors for several reasons. Sometimes the seed is so tiny (like wax begonias) that it needs the protection of an indoor environment to germinate and grow. Some small-seeded annuals may need as many as ten weeks to reach transplant size, so be sure to read the seed packet directions for the proper number of weeks needed to grow your transplants.

Another group of annuals may need to be started indoors in order to prolong the blooming season. For example, many marigolds thrive from direct-seeding, but they may not put on a decent show of color until midsummer. Starting seed indoors six weeks before outdoor planting will provide earlier color in the garden.

When starting seed of annuals indoors, you might consider both the one-step and the two-step method. The one-step system involves using pots filled with soil and planting a few seeds in each pot; it is most satisfactory when using seeds that are relatively large and easy to handle, such as zinnias and asters. Thin the resulting seedlings to one plant per pot, and when the plant is large enough to be set outdoors, remove the plant with its root ball and place it where you want it to flower.

The two-step system is best for tiny seeds, such as petunias and impatiens. It involves first germinating the seed in a seed tray, with the seeds scattered over the soil surface and lightly pressed into the soil to stop them from rolling around. Watering is done by misting because pressure from pouring water will disturb the seeds and hinder germination. The resulting seedlings are then lifted one at a time and transferred to individual pots to reach transplant size.

PREPARING THE SITE

Most annuals are not fussy about soil or fertilizer. As long as your soil drains well and receives six hours of sunlight a day, you can grow most of the flowering annuals featured in this book. Of course, you may need to water during dry spells; but, truthfully, annuals are the easiest of all flowers to grow.

Even if you have a shady site, there are colorful annuals to consider, including impatiens, browallia, coleus, and foxgloves. Removing some tree branches, or painting a dark wall white may be all you need to grow a wider selection of sun-loving annuals.

The best soil for annuals is called loam—especially sandy loam soil—since many of the most endearing annuals (such as marigolds and verbenas) come from semidesert areas. If your soil is too sandy and won't hold water or nutrients, add plenty of humus—especially well-decomposed animal manure, peat moss, garden compost, or leaf mold—to act as a sponge.

The opposite of sandy soil is clay soil. The greatest problem with clay is its impervious nature. It clumps together, puddles water on its surface, and acts as a barrier to plant roots. To improve clay soil, don't add sand—add plenty of humus or gypsum to act as an aerator.

Unlike many vegetables, annuals do not need large amounts of fertilizer. A light surface application of a general-purpose fertilizer raked into the top few centimeters of soil is normally sufficient to encourage beautiful flowering displays.

You should time your plantings to provide your annuals with the climatic conditions they prefer. Plant larkspur, snapdragons, and pansies even before the date of your last frost in spring, so they bloom before the heat of midsummer. Place your plants appropriately: portulaca will relish an open, dry, sunny border, while impatiens will prefer the cool, moist conditions that a shady, protected bed will provide.

PROBLEM SITES

If you have a particularly difficult planting site—such as the heavily alkaline soil common in limestone areas and desert regions, or a paved surface common in cities—then consider planting annuals in raised beds or containers, especially large tubs, urns, window boxes, and hanging baskets.

Raised beds are also the perfect solution to waterlogged soil that's difficult to drain. By laying down a foundation of crushed stone, making a frame from landscape ties, brick, or stones, and filling it with good topsoil purchased from a garden center, you can create a planting space raised above the water table.

When using containers to decorate a patio, terrace, or deck, be sure you have a tray underneath to collect water. In addition, ensure that each container has a drainage hole that is clog-resistant. In order to prevent soil from clogging a drainage hole, you should line the bottom of the container with broken pieces of clay pots or irregularly shaped stones.

The bigger the pot, the easier it will be to care for. Small pots, especially small hanging baskets, have a tendency to dry out quickly. Most container plantings will need watering every day, and it's helpful to use a long-handled watering wand attached to a garden hose so you can reach high into hanging baskets and window boxes or probe through dense foliage to reach the soil.

Avoid containers that may have a tendency to overheat, such as metal and plastic. Ceramic and wood are the preferred planter materials for sunny spots.

A good general-purpose soil mix for containers consists of three equal portions of good garden topsoil, peat moss or perlite, and sand. Packaged soil mixes suitable for house plants may be too light for containers used outdoors, where plants prefer a heavier soil that keeps them steady.

CARE BEFORE PLANTING

Many annuals will grow in impoverished soil. Some, such as nasturtiums and marigolds, may even produce too much leafy growth at the expense of flowers in an overly fertile soil. If you are a beginner gardener, new to a site, or are completely ignorant of the nature of your soil, then consider sending a soil sample to a soil laboratory to obtain a report. Any good nursery or garden center will tell you how to conduct a soil test. The report that comes back will tell you what nutrients are deficient in your soil for growing flowers and how to correct the deficiency. The report will also tell you how to correct any chemical imbalance, such as heavy alkalinity (usually corrected by adding sulphur) or heavy acidity (usually corrected by adding lime), and whether your soil needs the addition of any humus.

When buying transplants it is best to "buy green"—in other words, to start with a plant that has not yet produced flowers. Flowering transplants are often prone to transplant shock, or they have been subjected to some kind of abuse such as a cramped container, stretching to the light, or water starvation. A green transplant will usually overtake a flowering transplant and bloom for a longer period.

In addition, choose compact, bushy transplants over those that have grown tall and rangy. A compact transplant will produce more basal branches and create a better display than a tall plant that has been placed under stress.

If transplants have started to grow long, slender stems, pinch out the tips of the lead shoots. This will direct energy into producing side branches, creating a more pleasing shape.

If you buy transplants in peat pots, don't be tempted to plant them with the pot on the theory that the peat will quickly decompose. Instead, tear out the bottom of the pot so the roots have freedom to immediately grow down into the soil.

When removing a root ball from a plastic pot, gently tease apart the roots at the bottom and spread them apart in the planting hole. After filling the hole with soil, tamp the surface down so there is good contact between the soil and the roots.

CARE AFTER PLANTING

Unless natural rainfall has been forecasted, you should always water newly planted flower beds and continue to water whenever a week goes by without a drenching overnight rain. A good way to water flower beds is with a lawn sprinkler, allowing it to thoroughly soak the soil overnight.

Flower beds must be kept weed-free, and since hand-pulling weeds can be tedious, it is best to consider a weed-suffocating mulch. The most popular mulches for flower beds are decorative organic mulches, such as cocoa bean hulls, pine needles, wood chips, and shredded bark. The occasional weed may break through if the mulch is not thick enough, but these are easily spotted and removed by hand.

Black plastic is a popular mulch for cutting gardens, where plants are generally grown in straight rows: the plastic can be rolled out to cover a 3-foot (.9m) wide raised bed, anchored down along the edges with soil. A light layer of decorative organic mulch can be used to cover the plastic if it is aesthetically unattractive.

To keep annuals blooming, pick off faded flowers so they do not set seeds. The formation of seeds drains a plant of energy and will end its life sooner than if it is kept groomed or "dead-headed." Some annuals, such as triploid hybrid marigolds, are sterile and cannot set viable seed, so dead-heading is unnecessary.

PESTS AND DISEASES

Flowering annuals are not bothered by as many problem pests or diseases as vegetables, and it's possible to have a beautiful flower garden with just a few commonsense considerations. For example, if you are troubled by rabbits, rodents, or deer, instead of fencing in your property like vegetable gardeners do, you can use long-lasting sprays on flowering plants that make them extremely distasteful.

The most troublesome insect pests are slugs, snails, and beetles. Slugs and snails can be hand-picked in the early morning, or dishes of bait can be set among rows to kill them. Organic sprays of rotenone-pyrethrum will control many beetles without poisoning the soil, since rotenone and pyrethrum are both made from the powdered parts of tropical plants.

Nematodes are microscopic worms that can be extremely destructive in warmer areas with sandy soil. If a soil is badly infested with nematodes, a chemical drenching of the soil may be necessary, although certain flowers, such as marigolds, are resistant to nematodes.

The best protection against pests and diseases is good hygiene. Good soil encourages vigorous plants capable of resisting disease. Also, a thorough winter cleanup is essential. Pull up dead plants by the roots and rake up all old mulch and dead leaves, either burning them or relegating them to the compost pile so disease organisms and insect eggs cannot overwinter in a dormant state on garden debris.

DESIGNING WITH ANNUALS

Annuals are most often used in beds and borders in formal or informal designs. A bed is usually an island of soil surrounded by lawn, paving, or some other garden feature. Beds can be planted with a mass of flowers of all one kind and color (pink petunias, for example) or a mixture (red, white, and blue petunias, for example), or a combination of plants. When a combination of plants is used, care should be taken that they are approximately the same height or that tall plants are positioned in the middle and shorter plants are used as an edging around the perimeter. Sometimes a rainbow effect looks good, with different plants of different colors; other times a color theme is better, such as pink and red, blue and white, yellow and orange, or even all white, all blue, or all red. Beds usually have soil mounded in the middle to better display the plants.

A border is usually a strip of soil positioned against a wall, hedge, or fence. Tall plants are best placed at the back and shorter plants in front. Borders usually have soil sloping up towards the back in order to better display the plants.

Most plants grouped in beds or borders are best planted as informal "drifts," a mass of plants in an uneven shape, like a snow drift, each merging with the other to create a tapestry of color. However, plants can also be grouped to create geometric shapes such as squares, diamonds, and circles, providing a quiltlike appearance. Formal beds and borders usually have edges sharply outlined with bricks or trimmed hedges of boxwood.

Annuals are also useful in rock gardens and dry walls. A rock garden is usually planted on a gentle slope, accented with boulders and dwarf conifers to create an alpinelike "scree" (a natural boulder field). More sophisticated rock gardens have pools of water, streams, and cascades of water, with plants placed along the stream bank and pond margin. Although rock gardens can be planted entirely with annuals, they usually include some perennials and also flowering bulbs for maximum interest.

Though most flowering annuals are grown for garden display, many gardeners prefer to grow them for cutting to create beautiful fresh-flower and dried-flower arrangements indoors. Because a cutting garden can look rather sparse from having the flowers constantly harvested, many gardeners will have a special area reserved for cutting—often the cutting garden is combined with a vegetable garden, with alternating rows of flowers and vegetables. Even if a cutting garden is composed entirely of flowers, the most efficient layout is a system of straight rows or rectangular beds for easy access to each group of plants.

When designing a flower garden, consider whether it will be all annuals or a mixture of annuals, perennials, and bulbs; then lay out each border and bed on graph paper, with a square of the graph representing a specific amount of space in the garden. Using colored pens or pencils, shade in the colors you want and write in the plant's name. Generally speaking, you will need one plant per square foot (.09 sq m) of garden, so by counting the colored squares, you can plan ahead the number of plants needed.

Remember, too, that many annuals are climbing plants, suitable for creating a beautiful tall screen; so plan on taking color high into the sky with some vining annuals, such as moonflowers, morning glories, and black-eyed Susan vines. You can position a circle of wire, a trellis, or an arbor for the plants to climb up.

Tagetes erecta x *T. patula* 'Orange Fireworks' (triploid marigold)

THE ANNUALS

ABELMOSCHUS MOSCHATUS

COMMON NAME: Musk mallow

FAMILY: Malvaceae (Mallows)

DESCRIPTION: Native to India. Hibiscuslike 3- to 4-inch (8 to 10cm) flowers cover bushy, compact, spreading plants. Blooms last a day, but plants flower continuously all summer. Leaves are pointed, serrated, dark green.

HEIGHT: 15 inches (38cm).

COLOR: Mostly pink, white, red.

HARDINESS: Grows almost anywhere as a tender annual; prefers warm, sunny summers.

CULTURE: Prefers full sun, loam soil. Tolerates heat and drought. Start seed indoors 6 weeks before outdoor planting.

USES: Low beds, edging. Good patio pot plant.

AGERATUM HOUSTONIANUM

COMMON NAME: Ageratum; flossflower

FAMILY: Compositae (Daisies)

DESCRIPTION: Native to Mexico. Clusters of fluffy flowers occur continuously all summer, mostly on compact, mound-shaped plants with broad, rippled, pointed green leaves.

HEIGHT: 6 inches to 3 feet (15cm to .9m), depending on variety.

COLOR: Blue, purple, white.

HARDINESS: Killed by frost. Grows almost anywhere as a tender annual.

CULTURE: Prefers full sun, well-drained loam soil. Best grown from seed started indoors 8 weeks before outdoor planting.

USES: Edging beds and borders, containers. Tall kinds suitable for cutting.

AGROSTEMMA GITHAGO

COMMON NAME: Corn cockle

FAMILY: Caryophyllaceae (Carnations)

DESCRIPTION: Native to the Mediterranean region. Hibiscuslike 2-inch (5cm) flowers occur in summer on wispy, grasslike plants. Leaves are slender, pointed, gray-green.

HEIGHT: 2 to 3 feet (.6 to .9m).

COLOR: Pink with spotted throats.

HARDINESS: Moderately hardy, but killed by severe frost. Grows almost anywhere as a tender annual.

CULTURE: Prefers full sun, sandy or well-drained loam soil. Best grown from seed, direct-sown. Tolerates crowding.

USES: Beds, borders, meadow gardens, cutting.

ALCEA ROSEA

COMMON NAME: Hollyhock

FAMILY: Malvaceae (Mallows)

DESCRIPTION: Native to China. Hibiscus-type flowers cluster around tall flower spikes. Leaves are large, indented, dark green.

HEIGHT: 5 to 7 feet (1.5 to 2.1m).

COLOR: Red, pink, white, yellow, mahogany.

HARDINESS: Hardy perennial; several kinds may be treated as annuals. Annual kinds grow almost anywhere.

CULTURE: Prefers full sun, well-drained loam soil. Best grown from seed started indoors 6 weeks before outdoor planting.

USES: Tall backgrounds for beds and borders.

AMARANTHUS CAUDATUS

COMMON NAME: Love-lies-bleeding

FAMILY: Amaranthaceae (Amaranthus)

DESCRIPTION: Native to Mexico. Long, arching flower clusters resemble ropes; they contrast against the pointed, lancelike, bright green leaves.

HEIGHT: 3 to 5 feet (.9 to 1.5m).

COLOR: Red.

HARDINESS: Killed by frost. Grows almost anywhere as a tender annual.

CULTURE: Prefers full sun, well-drained loam soil. Best grown from seed, direct-sown.

USES: Beds, borders, containers, cutting.

AMARANTHUS TRICOLOR

COMMON NAME: Joseph's-coat

FAMILY: Amaranthaceae (Amaranthus)

DESCRIPTION: Native to Mexico. Grown for its colorful, arching crown of leaves. Lower leaves are spear-shaped, green or bronze.

HEIGHT: 3 to 4 feet (.9 to 1.2m).

COLOR: Combinations of red, yellow, orange, green, chocolate.

HARDINESS: Killed by frost. Grows almost anywhere as a tender annual.

CULTURE: Prefers full sun, well-drained loam soil. Best grown from seed, direct-sown.

USES: Beds, borders, tall backgrounds.

AMMI MAJUS

COMMON NAME: Bishop's weed

FAMILY: Umbelliferae (Carrots)

DESCRIPTION: Native to Europe. Resembles Queen-Anne's-lace but is more billowing in its habit. Slender, branching stems bear finely cut leaves and flat flower clusters.

HEIGHT: To 2½ feet (.8m).

COLOR: White.

HARDINESS: Killed by frost. Grows almost anywhere as a tender annual.

CULTURE: Prefers full sun, loam soil. Best grown from seed, direct-sown after frost danger. Cover seeds with soil sufficient to anchor them. Flowers for about 4 weeks in summer. Tolerates crowding.

USES: Mostly used in cutting gardens, but also mixes well in perennial borders to give a misty look among more domineering plants.

ANAGALLIS MONELLI

COMMON NAME: Blue pimpernel

FAMILY: Primulaceae (Primroses)

DESCRIPTION: Native to the Mediterranean region. Mound-shaped plants resemble forget-me-nots. Leaves are slender, lancelike.

HEIGHT: 12 inches (31cm).

COLOR: Deep blue.

HARDINESS: Mostly grown in coastal gardens and wherever a cool summer climate encourages spectacular flowering.

CULTURE: Prefers full sun, sandy or well-drained loam soil. Direct-sow, or start seed 6 weeks before outdoor planting. Blooms best when nights are cool.

USES: Edging beds and borders.

ANCHUSA CAPENSIS

COMMON NAME: Summer forget-me-not

FAMILY: Boraginaceae (Borages)

DESCRIPTION: Native to South Africa. Though biennial, some varieties can be grown as annuals. Flowers resemble forget-me-nots. Borne on low-mounded plants with slender, lancelike leaves.

HEIGHT: 12 inches (31cm).

COLOR: Blue.

HARDINESS: Hardy annual. Grows best where summers are cool.

CULTURE: Prefers full sun, sandy or well-drained loam soil. Start seed indoors 6 to 8 weeks before outdoor planting.

USES: Edging beds and borders, container plantings.

ANETHUM GRAVEOLENS

COMMON NAME: Dill

FAMILY: Umbelliferae (Carrots)

DESCRIPTION: Native to the Mediterranean region. Grows erect, branching stems with finely cut, feathery, gray-green leaves and flat flower clusters resembling Queen-Anne's-lace. Summer-flowering. All parts of the plant, including the seeds, are aromatic.

HEIGHT: Up to 4 feet (1.2m).

COLOR: Yellow.

HARDINESS: Killed by frost. Grows almost anywhere as a tender annual.

CULTURE: Direct-sow, covering seeds just enough to anchor them. Prefers full sun, good drainage. Tolerates crowding.

USES: Good tall accent and background for mixed beds and borders. Popular cut flower, especially as a dried everlasting. Used extensively in herb gardens.

ANTIRRHINUM MAJUS

COMMON NAME: Snapdragon

FAMILY: Scrophulariaceae (Figworts)

DESCRIPTION: Native to the Mediterranean region. Tubular flowers, some with closed mouths, others with open throats, cluster around an erect spike. Leaves are lancelike, dark green.

HEIGHT: 2 to 4 feet (.6 to 1.2m).

COLOR: Red, pink, yellow, orange, white, bicolors.

HARDINESS: Hardy annual. Grows almost anywhere, flowering best when nights are cool.

CULTURE: Prefers full sun, sandy or well-drained loam soil. Best grown from seed started indoors 8 weeks before outdoor planting. Tall varieties need staking.

USES: Tall backgrounds for beds and borders. Short kinds good for containers. Excellent cut flower.

AQUILEGIA 'MCKANA GIANTS'

COMMON NAME: Columbine

FAMILY: Ranunculaceae (Buttercups)

DESCRIPTION: Native to North America. Hybrids of perennial species are best grown as annuals from seed started early. Pendant, tubular flowers have long spurs and are held erect above lacy gray-green foliage.

HEIGHT: 2 to 3 feet (.6 to .9m).

COLOR: White, blue, pink, yellow, red, bicolors.

HARDINESS: Grows almost anywhere as a tender annual.

CULTURE: Prefers full sun in cool areas, some shade in warm areas, in sandy or well-drained loam soil. Start seed indoors 8 weeks before outdoor planting after frost danger.

USES: Mixed beds and borders. Excellent for cutting.

ARCTOTIS STOECHADIFOLIA

COMMON NAME: African daisy

FAMILY: Compositae (Daisies)

DESCRIPTION: Native to South Africa. Shimmering daisylike flowers up to 3 inches (7.5cm) across occur in midsummer on slender stems above a rosette of toothed green leaves.

HEIGHT: 18 inches (46cm).

COLOR: Red, purple, pink, yellow, orange, white, bicolors.

HARDINESS: Killed by frost. Grows almost anywhere as a tender annual, flowering when nights are cool.

CULTURE: Prefers full sun, sandy or well-drained loam soil. Best grown from seed, direct-sown.

USES: Beds, borders, meadow gardens, cutting.

BEGONIA × *SEMPERFLORENS-CULTORUM*

COMMON NAME: Wax begonia

FAMILY: Begoniaceae (Begonias)

DESCRIPTION: Derived from species native to South America. Four-petaled flowers up to 1 inch (2.5cm) across occur all summer on bushy plants. Rounded, wavy, green or bronze leaves have a waxlike sheen.

HEIGHT: 1 to 2.5 feet (.3 to .8m).

COLOR: White, red, pink, rose, bicolors.

HARDINESS: Killed by frost. Grows almost anywhere as a tender annual.

CULTURE: Hybrids grow in sun or shade. Prefers cool, moist, humus-rich soil. Best grown from seed started indoors 10 weeks before outdoor planting.

USES: Beds, borders, edging, windowboxes, hanging baskets, other container plantings.

BETA VULGARIS var. *CICLA*

COMMON NAME: Chard (ornamental)

FAMILY: Chenopodiaceae (Goosefoots)

DESCRIPTION: Native to Europe. Leafy plants grown for their colorful, upright, edible stems and savoy leaves.

HEIGHT: 3 feet (.9m).

COLOR: The highly ornamental stems can be white, red, pink, or orange.

HARDINESS: Hardy biennial mostly grown as a hardy annual. Grows almost anywhere.

CULTURE: Prefers full sun in sandy or well-drained loam soil. Direct-sow.

USES: The red variety is a valuable component of all-red gardens. Especially attractive planted in containers.

BORAGO OFFICINALIS

COMMON NAME: Borage

FAMILY: Boraginaceae (Borages)

DESCRIPTION: Native to the Mediterranean region. Plants have blue-green leaves covered with silvery hairs and starlike flowers. Oblong leaves emit a cucumber fragrance.

HEIGHT: 2 feet (.6m).

COLOR: Blue.

HARDINESS: Killed by frost. Grows almost anywhere as a tender annual.

CULTURE: Prefers full sun, loam soil, good drainage. Direct-sow.

USES: Mixed beds and borders. Attractive to bees. Mostly used in herb gardens.

BRACHYCOME IBERIDIFOLIA

COMMON NAME: Swan River daisy

FAMILY: Compositae (Daisies)

DESCRIPTION: Native to Australia. Daisylike 1-inch (2.5cm) flowers bloom in summer, creating a mounded plant. Leaves are narrow, indented, dark green.

HEIGHT: 12 inches (31cm).

COLOR: Blue, white.

HARDINESS: Killed by frost. Grows almost anywhere as a tender annual. Flowers best during cool nights.

CULTURE: Prefers full sun, sandy or well-drained loam soil. Best grown from seed started indoors 6 weeks before outdoor planting.

USES: Beds, borders, containers.

BRASSICA OLERACEA var. *ACEPHALA*

COMMON NAME: Ornamental kale

FAMILY: Cruciferae (Cabbages)

DESCRIPTION: Native to Europe. Plants resemble cabbage or kale, with blue-green outer leaves and a frilly center of a contrasting color.

HEIGHT: 12 inches (31cm).

COLOR: White, pink, red.

HARDINESS: Killed only by a hard freeze. Grows almost anywhere as a hardy annual, but produces its best colors during cool weather.

CULTURE: Prefers full sun and sandy or well-drained loam soil. Start seed indoors 6 weeks before outdoor planting, timing outdoor plantings so that plants mature during cool weather (60 days after sowing). Mostly grown for autumn and winter color.

USES: Massing in beds and borders, containers.

BRIZA MAXIMA

COMMON NAME: Big quaking grass

FAMILY: Gramineae (Grasses)

DESCRIPTION: Native to the Mediterranean region. Plants grow clumps of slender green leaves that turn russet shades and masses of nodding papery flower heads that resemble hops.

HEIGHT: 2 to 3 feet (.6 to .9m).

COLOR: Gray-green flower heads turn brown.

HARDINESS: Killed by frost. Grows almost anywhere as a hardy annual.

CULTURE: Prefers full sun and sandy or well-drained loam soil. Direct-sow into garden soil. Tolerates crowding.

USES: Good highlight for mixed beds and borders. Valued for dried arrangements.

BROWALLIA SPECIOSA

COMMON NAME: Blue bells, bush violet

FAMILY: Solanaceae (Nightshades)

DESCRIPTION: Native to South America. The trumpet-shaped flowers are freely produced all summer on mounded, spreading plants, sometimes almost hiding the spear-shaped bright green leaves.

HEIGHT: 18 inches (46cm).

COLOR: Blue, white.

HARDINESS: Killed by frost. Grows almost anywhere as a tender annual, flowering best when nights are cool.

CULTURE: Prefers a lightly shaded location and a high-humus soil with good drainage. Start seed indoors 8 weeks before outdoor planting.

USES: Temporary ground cover, edging, hanging baskets, window boxes, other container plantings.

CALCEOLARIA INTEGRIFOLIA

COMMON NAME: Pocketbook flower

FAMILY: Scrophulariaceae (Figworts)

DESCRIPTION: Native to South America. Bushy plants grow serrated, heart-shaped, dark green leaves and pouch-shaped flowers, ½ inch (13mm) across.

HEIGHT: 12 inches (31cm).

COLOR: Canary yellow.

HARDINESS: Moderately hardy annual. Killed by severe frost. Flowers best where summers are cool.

CULTURE: Prefers full sun, sandy or well-drained loam soil. Best grown from seed started indoors 8 to 10 weeks before outdoor planting.

USES: Massing in beds and borders; containers.

CALENDULA OFFICINALIS

COMMON NAME: Pot marigold

FAMILY: Compositae (Daisies)

DESCRIPTION: Native to southern Europe. Double 3-inch (7.5cm) daisylike flowers occur continuously all summer on bushy plants. Light green, spear-shaped leaves release a spicy fragrance when bruised.

HEIGHT: 18 inches (46cm).

COLOR: Orange, yellow, white.

HARDINESS: Grows almost anywhere as a hardy annual. Self-seeds readily.

CULTURE: Prefers full sun, good drainage, cool nights. Best grown from seed, direct-sown.

USES: Beds, borders, cutting, container plantings. Popular in herb gardens.

CALLISTEPHUS CHINENSIS

COMMON NAME: China aster

FAMILY: Compositae (Daisies)

DESCRIPTION: Native to China. Daisylike flowers up to 5 inches (13cm) across, mostly doubled, are borne on upright stems in midsummer. Leaves are indented, dark green.

HEIGHT: 1½ to 3 feet (.5 to .9m).

COLOR: Red, white, blue, purple, pink.

HARDINESS: Killed by frost. Grows almost anywhere as a tender annual.

CULTURE: Prefers full sun, well-drained loam soil. Best grown from seed, direct-sown.

USES: Beds, borders, cutting.

CAMPANULA MEDIUM

COMMON NAME: Canterbury-bells

FAMILY: Campanulaceae (Bellflowers)

DESCRIPTION: Native to southern Europe. Cup-shaped flowers up to 3 inches (7.5cm) across are grouped around a slender stem. Leaves are slender, smooth, pointed.

HEIGHT: 3 feet (.9m).

COLOR: Blue, pink, white.

HARDINESS: Does best where summers are cool. A biennial grown mostly as a hardy annual in cool, coastal gardens.

CULTURE: Prefers full sun, good drainage. Start seed early indoors and transplant 10-week-old seedlings to the garden. Blooms in 6 months from seed when nights are cool. Plants generally need staking to keep them erect.

USES: Mixed beds and borders.

CANNA 'HYBRID TROPICAL ROSE'

COMMON NAME: Annual canna

FAMILY: Cannaceae (Cannas)

DESCRIPTION: Developed in Japan from species native to South America. Erect stems are sheathed with broad, bronzy, bananalike leaves, topped with a spike of gladioluslike flowers.

HEIGHT: Up to 3 feet (.9m).

COLOR: Rose-pink.

HARDINESS: Tender perennial best grown as a tender annual. Dies after frost but forms corms that can be stored indoors and replanted the following spring.

CULTURE: Prefers full sun, sandy or loam soil. Start seed indoors 8 weeks before outdoor planting, soaking the hard pea-size seeds first overnight in lukewarm water to aid germination.

USES: Massing in beds and borders.

CAPSICUM ANNUUM

COMMON NAME: Ornamental pepper

FAMILY: Solanaceae (Nightshades)

DESCRIPTION: Native to South America. Star-shaped white flowers produce ornamental round or pointed fruits, depending on variety. Smooth, lancelike, dark green leaves form bushy plants.

HEIGHT: 1 to 3 feet (.3 to .9m).

COLOR: Fruits are mostly red, yellow, orange.

HARDINESS: Killed by frost. Grows almost anywhere as a tender annual.

CULTURE: Prefers full sun, well-drained loam soil. Best grown from seed started indoors 6 to 8 weeks before outdoor planting.

USES: Beds, borders, edging, containers.

CARTHAMUS TINCTORIUS

COMMON NAME: False saffron

FAMILY: Compositae (Daisies)

DESCRIPTION: Native to the Mediterranean region. Erect thistlelike plants with prickly, sharply indented green leaves and thimble-sized flowers.

HEIGHT: Up to 3 feet (.9m).

COLOR: Orange.

HARDINESS: Killed by frost. Grows almost anywhere as a tender annual.

CULTURE: Prefers full sun, sandy or well-drained loam soil. Direct-sow after frost danger, covering seeds with just enough soil to anchor them.

USES: Mostly used in clumps as an ornamental in herb gardens. The plants yield an edible oil and natural dye.

CATHARANTHUS ROSEUS

COMMON NAME: Vinca; Madagascar periwinkle

FAMILY: Apocynaceae (Dogbanes)

DESCRIPTION: Native to Madagascar. Star-shaped flowers cover low, spreading plants with oval, pointed, glossy green leaves.

HEIGHT: 9 to 12 inches (23 to 31cm).

COLOR: Red, pink, purple, white, bicolors.

HARDINESS: Killed by frost. Grows almost anywhere as a tender annual.

CULTURE: Prefers full sun, sandy or well-drained loam soil. Heat- and drought-tolerant. Best grown from seed started indoors 8 weeks before outdoor planting.

USES: Temporary ground cover, beds, borders, containers.

CELOSIA ARGENTEA var. *CRISTATA*

COMMON NAME: Crested cockscomb

FAMILY: Amaranthaceae (Amaranthus)

DESCRIPTION: Native to India. The flower head resembles a clump of brain coral. Leaves are lancelike on erect stems, bright green or bronze.

HEIGHT: 1 to 3 feet (.3 to .9m).

COLOR: Red, pink, orange, yellow.

HARDINESS: Killed by frost. Grows almost anywhere as a tender annual. Grows best where summers are warm and sunny.

CULTURE: Prefers full sun, well-drained loam soil. Best grown from seed, direct-sown; resents transplanting.

USES: Beds, borders, cutting. Popular for drying.

CELOSIA PLUMOSA

COMMON NAME: Plumed cockscomb; prince's feather

FAMILY: Amaranthaceae (Amaranthus)

DESCRIPTION: Native to Asia. Silky flower plumes are borne all summer on upright stems. Leaves are lancelike, bright green or bronze.

HEIGHT: 1 to 3 feet (.3 to .9m).

COLOR: Red, pink, orange, yellow.

HARDINESS: Killed by frost. Grows almost anywhere as a tender annual. Grows best where summers are warm and sunny.

CULTURE: Prefers full sun, well-drained loam soil. Best grown from seed, direct-sown; resents transplanting.

USES: Beds, borders, cutting. Popular for drying.

CENTAUREA CYANUS

COMMON NAME: Bachelor's-button; cornflower

FAMILY: Compositae (Daisies)

DESCRIPTION: Native to Europe. Double 1½- to 2-inch (4 to 5cm) flowers grow on long, slender stems and bloom in summer. Slender, gray-green leaves create bushy plants.

HEIGHT: 2 to 3 feet (.6 to .9m).

COLOR: Red, white, blue, mahogany.

HARDINESS: Grows almost anywhere as a hardy annual. Self-seeds readily.

CULTURE: Prefers full sun, sandy or well-drained loam soil. Best grown from seed, direct-sown.

USES: Beds, borders, cutting, meadow gardens.

CENTAUREA MOSCHATA

COMMON NAME: Sweet-sultan

FAMILY: Compositae (Daisies)

DESCRIPTION: Native to the Mediterranean region. Plants resemble bachelor's-buttons, with slender, indented leaves and 3-inch (7.5cm) flowers, fragrant, predominantly in pastel shades. Summer-flowering.

HEIGHT: 2½ feet (.8m).

COLOR: White, pink, lilac, purple, yellow.

HARDINESS: Moderately hardy annual, killed by severe frost. Flowers best where summers are cool.

CULTURE: Prefers full sun; tolerates impoverished soil. Direct-sow seeds into sandy or well-drained loam soil.

USES: Mixed beds and borders. Exquisite cut flower.

CHEIRANTHUS CHEIRI

COMMON NAME: English wallflower

FAMILY: Cruciferae (Cabbages)

DESCRIPTION: Native to Europe. Plants form erect stems with clusters of four-petaled, fragrant flowers during cool conditions. Leaves are slender, lancelike, dark green.

HEIGHT: 2 feet (.6m).

COLOR: White, cream, yellow, orange, mahogany, purple, pink, rose.

HARDINESS: Most varieties are hardy biennials that must be overwintered in a mild-winter region to bloom in early spring the following year. However, varieties are available that can be treated as annuals.

CULTURE: Demands cool conditions throughout its growing period, full sun, good drainage. Start annual varieties from seed in March to flower in August and September.

USES: Massing in beds and borders.

CHRYSANTHEMUM CARINATUM

COMMON NAME: Painted daisy; tricolor chrysanthemum

FAMILY: Compositae (Daisies)

DESCRIPTION: Native to Morocco. Erect bushy plants produce 3½-inch (9cm) daisylike flowers during cool nights. Leaves are feathery, dark green.

HEIGHT: 3 feet (.9m).

COLOR: Yellow, red, pink, white, bicolors.

HARDINESS: Hardy annual that flowers best in areas with cool summers.

CULTURE: Prefers full sun, sandy or well-drained loam soil, cool nights. Best grown from seed, direct-sown.

USES: Beds, borders, cutting, wildflower meadows.

CHRYSANTHEMUM CORONARIUM

COMMON NAME: Garland chrysanthemum; crown daisy

FAMILY: Compositae (Daisies)

DESCRIPTION: Native to North Africa. Bushy, branching plants are covered with bright 1½-inch (4cm) daisylike flowers finely indented.

HEIGHT: Up to 2½ feet (.8m).

COLOR: Mostly yellow, cream, white, bicolors.

HARDINESS: Tolerates mild frost. Grows almost anywhere as a hardy annual.

CULTURE: Direct-sow in early spring, covering seeds with just enough soil to anchor them. Prefers full sun and cool nights to bloom well. Late summer sowings may bloom in autumn.

USES: Mixed beds and borders, wildflower meadow mixtures, cutting. Combines well with red Shirley poppies. Good for coastal gardens.

CHRYSANTHEMUM MAXIMUM

COMMON NAME: Shasta daisy

FAMILY: Compositae (Daisies)

DESCRIPTION: Special dwarf hybrids have been developed from perennial species native to Europe to bloom the first year from seed. The bushy, mound-shaped plants produce masses of 2½-inch (6.5cm) daisylike flowers. Leaves are lancelike, dark green.

HEIGHT: 12 inches (31cm).

COLOR: White with yellow centers.

HARDINESS: Grows almost anywhere as a hardy annual. May survive freezing winter to rebloom as a perennial.

CULTURE: Prefers full sun, well-drained loam soil, cool nights. Best grown from seed started indoors 10 weeks before outdoor planting.

USES: Beds, borders, containers.

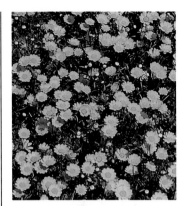

CHRYSANTHEMUM MULTICAULE

COMMON NAME: Corn marigold

FAMILY: Compositae (Daisies)

DESCRIPTION: Native to North America. Mounded plants grow masses of 1½-inch (4cm) daisylike flowers and finely indented, green leaves.

HEIGHT: Up to 18 inches (46cm).

COLOR: Bright golden yellow.

HARDINESS: Killed by frost. Grows almost anywhere as a tender annual.

CULTURE: Prefers full sun and sandy or well-drained loam soil. Direct-sow in early spring after frost danger. Flowers in early summer; blooms best when nights are cool.

USES: Massing in beds and borders; good for edging, rock gardens, wild-flower meadow mixtures. Especially good for containers, including window boxes.

CHRYSANTHEMUM PARTHENIUM

COMMON NAME: Feverfew

FAMILY: Compositae (Daisies)

DESCRIPTION: Native to Europe. Plants create a cloudlike mass of delicate, aromatic stems and narrow, pointed leaves. Tiny, ¾-inch (19mm), daisylike flowers cover the plants.

HEIGHT: 2 to 3 feet (.6 to .9m).

COLOR: White or pale yellow with yellow centers.

HARDINESS: Hardy perennial; will flower the first year as a hardy annual if seed is started early indoors.

CULTURE: Prefers full sun, good drainage, cool nights; tolerates impoverished soil providing drainage is good. Direct-sow or start seed indoors 8 weeks before outdoor planting.

USES: Mixed beds and borders, herb gardens.

CHRYSANTHEMUM PTARMICIFLORUM

COMMON NAME: Dusty-miller

FAMILY: Compositae (Daisies)

DESCRIPTION: Developed from species native to Africa. One of several plants known as dusty-millers because of their distinctive silvery blue leaves.

HEIGHT: 1 to 2 feet (.3 to .6m).

COLOR: Flowers are small, yellow; of no ornamental value.

HARDINESS: Killed by severe frost. Grows almost anywhere as a moderately hardy annual.

CULTURE: Prefers full sun, good drainage. Start seed indoors 10 weeks before outdoor planting.

USES: Massing in beds, edging borders, mixing with other annuals in container plantings.

CLARKIA AMOENA

COMMON NAME: Godetia; satin flower

FAMILY: Onagraceae (Evening primroses)

DESCRIPTION: Native to California. Mostly four-petaled, shimmering flowers bloom in early summer on low, spreading plants with lancelike green leaves.

HEIGHT: 12 inches (31cm).

COLOR: Red, pink, purple, white, bicolors.

HARDINESS: Hardy annual. Grows best in areas with cool summers, especially coastal locations.

CULTURE: Prefers full sun, sandy or well-drained loam soil, cool nights. Best grown from seed, direct-sown.

USES: Beds, borders.

*CLARKIA UNGUICULATA (*also *CLARKIA ELEGANS)*

COMMON NAME: Clarkia

FAMILY: Onagraceae (Evening primroses)

DESCRIPTION: Native to California. Tall, slender flower spikes grow carnationlike flowers all along the stem. Leaves are indented.

HEIGHT: 2½ feet (.8m).

COLOR: White, pink, red, salmon, lavender, purple.

HARDINESS: Can be grown almost anywhere as a hardy annual, with flowering timed for cool weather.

CULTURE: Prefers full sun, well-drained soil. Direct-sow as early in spring as possible so flowering occurs while nights are still cool. Allow 10 weeks to flowering.

USES: Mostly grown for cutting.

CLEOME HASSLERANA

COMMON NAME: Spider flower

FAMILY: Capparaceae (Capers)

DESCRIPTION: Native to Central America. Clusters of ½-inch (13mm) flowers create a ball shape atop a continually elongating flower stem. Serrated oval leaves are arranged in a fan shape.

HEIGHT: 4 to 5 feet (1.2 to 1.5m).

COLOR: Pink, purple, white.

HARDINESS: Killed by frost. Grows almost anywhere as a tender annual.

CULTURE: Prefers full sun, sandy or well-drained loam soil. Best grown from seed, direct-sown. Does well where summers are warm and sunny.

USES: Tall backgrounds for beds and borders.

COBAEA SCANDENS

COMMON NAME: Cup-and-saucer vine

FAMILY: Polemoniaceae (Phlox)

DESCRIPTION: Native to Central America. Cup-shaped flowers bloom all summer on fast-growing vines with smooth, oval green leaves.

HEIGHT: 10 feet (3m).

COLOR: Purple, pink, white.

HARDINESS: Killed by frost. Grows almost anywhere as a tender annual.

CULTURE: Prefers full sun, loam soil. Best grown from seed started indoors 6 to 8 weeks before outdoor planting. Needs strong support.

USES: Vine for screening.

COIX LACRYMA-JOBI

COMMON NAME: Job's-tears

FAMILY: Gramineae (Grasses)

DESCRIPTION: Native to Indonesia. Plants grow a fountain of broad, swordlike green leaves and heavy, arching flower spikes with ornamental green seeds that resemble teardrops.

HEIGHT: 3 to 4 feet (.9 to 1.2m).

COLOR: Male flowers are yellow and inconspicuous. Female flowers on same floral cluster produce beadlike green kernels.

HARDINESS: Killed by frost. Grows almost anywhere as a tender annual.

CULTURE: Prefers full sun, good drainage. Start seed indoors 6 weeks before outdoor planting.

USES: A good highlight used sparingly in mixed beds and borders. Valued for dried arrangements.

COLEUS BLUMEI

COMMON NAME: Flame nettle; painted nettle

FAMILY: Labiatae (Mints)

DESCRIPTION: Native to Indonesia. Nettlelike, heart-shaped serrated leaves are multicolored and followed by unattractive slender blue flower spikes.

HEIGHT: 2 to 3 feet (.6 to .9m).

COLOR: Grown for its decorative leaves in combinations of yellow, lime green, red, orange, chocolate.

HARDINESS: Killed by frost. Grows almost anywhere as a tender annual.

CULTURE: Prefers lightly shaded, cool, moist soil. Best grown from seed started indoors 10 weeks before outdoor planting. Softwood cuttings also root easily.

USES: Beds, borders, window boxes, hanging baskets, other containers.

CONSOLIDA AMBIGUA *(also DELPHINIUM AJACIS)*

COMMON NAME: Rocket larkspur

FAMILY: Ranunculaceae (Buttercups)

DESCRIPTION: Native to the Mediterranean region; naturalized in California. Slender spikes are densely set with 1-inch (2.5cm) double florets. Leaves are indented.

HEIGHT: 2 feet (.6m).

COLOR: Blue mostly, but white and pink offered in mixtures.

HARDINESS: Can be grown almost anywhere as a hardy annual if flowering is timed for cool weather. Allow 10 weeks from seed to flowering.

CULTURE: Prefers full sun, good drainage, cool nights. Direct-sow in spring for summer flowering; autumn for spring flowering.

USES: Tall backgrounds, cutting, wildflower meadows.

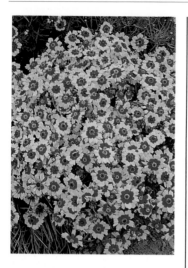

COREOPSIS TINCTORIA

COMMON NAME: Calliopsis

FAMILY: Compositae (Daisies)

DESCRIPTION: Native to North America. Wispy plants produce masses of daisylike flowers. Leaves are narrow, pointed, green.

HEIGHT: 1 to 2 feet (.3 to .6m).

COLOR: Red, orange, yellow, mahogany, bicolors.

HARDINESS: Grows almost anywhere as a hardy annual.

CULTURE: Prefers full sun, sandy or well-drained loam soil. Best grown from seed, direct-sown.

USES: Beds, borders, cutting, meadow gardens.

COSMOS BIPINNATUS

COMMON NAME: Common cosmos

FAMILY: Compositae (Daisies)

DESCRIPTION: Native to Mexico. Tall, slender plants have feathery foliage. Flowers up to 4 inches (10cm) across are mostly single and are produced continuously all summer.

HEIGHT: 4 to 5 feet (1.2 to 1.5m).

COLOR: Red, pink, white.

HARDINESS: Killed by frost. Grows almost anywhere as a tender annual.

CULTURE: Prefers full sun, sandy or well-drained loam soil. Best grown from seed, direct-sown. Generally needs staking.

USES: Tall backgrounds for beds and borders, cutting.

COSMOS SULPHUREUS

COMMON NAME: Yellow cosmos

FAMILY: Compositae (Daisies)

DESCRIPTION: Native to Mexico. Bushy, spreading growth habit. Flowers are mostly semidouble up to 2 inches (5cm) across; occur continuously all summer. Leaves are narrow, pointed, green.

HEIGHT: 1½ to 3 feet (.5 to .9m).

COLOR: Yellow, orange, flame red.

HARDINESS: Killed by frost. Grows almost anywhere as a tender annual.

CULTURE: Prefers full sun, sandy or well-drained loam soil. Better heat and drought tolerance than common cosmos. Best grown from seed, direct-sown.

USES: Beds, borders, cutting. Dwarf types suitable for containers.

CUCURBITA PEPO var. *OVIFERA*

COMMON NAME: Ornamental small gourds

FAMILY: Cucurbitaceae (Cucumbers)

DESCRIPTION: Native to South and Central America. Plants grow cucumberlike vines that have tendrils for climbing. Star-shaped yellow flowers grow into decorative fruits shaped like eggs, lemons, and pears.

HEIGHT: 10 feet (3m).

COLOR: White, green, yellow, orange, bicolors.

HARDINESS: Killed by frost. Grows almost anywhere as a tender annual.

CULTURE: Prefers full sun, sandy or well-drained loam soil. Heat-tolerant. Best grown from seed, direct-sown. Needs staking.

USES: Temporary screen; fruits are suitable for drying.

CYNARA CARDUNCULUS

COMMON NAME: Cardoon

FAMILY: Compositae (Daisies)

DESCRIPTION: Native to the Mediterranean region. Tall thistlelike plants have silvery, sharply indented leaves. Erect flower stems are topped with thistlelike flowers. Branching habit.

HEIGHT: Up to 12 feet (3.7m).

COLOR: Pink, but grown mostly for its ornamental silvery green, prickly leaves.

HARDINESS: Killed by frost. Grows almost anywhere as a tender annual. Perennial in frost-free areas.

CULTURE: Needs full sun, fertile loam or sandy soil, good drainage. Can be direct-sown, but is usually transplanted in cold-winter areas.

USES: Tall background accent in mixed beds and borders. Popular ornamental in herb gardens because young stalks, if blanched, have a pleasant celerylike flavor.

CYNOGLOSSUM AMABILE

COMMON NAME: Chinese forget-me-not

FAMILY: Boraginaceae (Borages)

DESCRIPTION: Native to China. Masses of forget-me-not flowers occur in summer on bushy plants. Leaves are narrow, pointed, green.

HEIGHT: 2 feet (.6m).

COLOR: Blue, white.

HARDINESS: Grows almost anywhere as a hardy annual.

CULTURE: Prefers full sun, well-drained loam soil. Best grown from seed, direct-sown.

USES: Beds, borders, cutting.

DAHLIA × HYBRIDA

COMMON NAME: Bedding dahlia

FAMILY: Compositae (Daisies)

DESCRIPTION: Developed from species native to Mexico. Shimmering daisylike single and double flowers up to 4 inches (10cm) across flower continuously all summer on upright, succulent stems. Leaves are indented, bright green or bronze.

HEIGHT: 2 to 3 feet (.6 to .9m).

COLOR: Red, pink, purple, yellow, orange, white.

HARDINESS: Killed by frost. Grows almost anywhere as a tender annual.

CULTURE: Prefers full sun, sandy or well-drained loam soil, cool nights. Best grown from seed started indoors 6 to 8 weeks before outdoor planting.

USES: Beds, borders, cutting.

DATURA METEL

COMMON NAME: Thorn apple; angel's trumpet

FAMILY: Solanaceae (Nightshades)

DESCRIPTION: Native to South America. Fragrant trumpet-shaped, 4-inch (10cm) flowers bloom all summer on spreading plants. Leaves are broad, spear-shaped, coarse-textured. All parts of this plant are poisonous.

HEIGHT: 3 feet (.9m).

COLOR: White.

HARDINESS: Killed by frost. Grows almost anywhere as a tender annual.

CULTURE: Prefers full sun, sandy or well-drained loam soil. Best grown from seed started indoors 6 weeks before outdoor planting.

USES: Beds, borders, pots.

DAUCUS CAROTA var. CAROTA

COMMON NAME: Queen-Anne's-lace

FAMILY: Umbelliferae (Carrots)

DESCRIPTION: Origin unsure; probably southeastern Europe. Naturalized in meadows all across Europe and North America. Lacy, flat flowers up to 5 inches (13cm) across are held erect on tall stems; leaves are feathery. Summer-flowering.

HEIGHT: 3 to 4 feet (.9 to 1.2m).

COLOR: White.

HARDINESS: Grows almost anywhere as a hardy annual.

CULTURE: Tolerates impoverished soil providing drainage is good. Best grown from seed, direct-sown in full sun.

USES: Mostly used in cutting gardens and meadow plantings, mixed with blue cornflowers and blue wild chicory.

DELPHINIUM × CULTORUM

COMMON NAME: Delphinium

FAMILY: Ranunculaceae (Buttercups)

DESCRIPTION: Native to northern Europe. Tall flower spikes are studded with 2-inch (5cm) florets, with a cluster of smaller petals at the center called a "bee." Leaves are broad, deeply notched.

HEIGHT: 3 to 5 feet (.9 to 1.5m).

COLOR: Blue, pink, purple, white.

HARDINESS: Hardy perennial grown as an annual. Flowers best where summers are cool.

CULTURE: Prefers full sun, well-drained loam soil, cool nights. Best grown from seed started indoors 10 to 12 weeks before outdoor planting. Usually needs staking.

USES: Tall backgrounds for beds and borders, cutting.

DIANTHUS BARBATUS

COMMON NAME: Sweet William

FAMILY: Caryophyllaceae (Carnations)

DESCRIPTION: Native to Europe and Asia. Most sweet Williams are biennials, but certain kinds such as 'Wee Willie' will bloom the first year from seed started early. Unlike the tall biennial variety, plants are low-growing with lancelike leaves.

HEIGHT: 12 inches (31cm).

COLOR: White, red, pink, mahogany, purple. Most have contrasting "eyes."

HARDINESS: Prefers full sun; sandy, well-drained soil. Start seed indoors 8 weeks before outdoor planting.

CULTURE: Hardy biennial that can be grown as a hardy annual.

USES: Edging beds and borders, rock gardens.

DIANTHUS CARYOPHYLLUS

COMMON NAME: Carnation

FAMILY: Caryophyllaceae (Carnations)

DESCRIPTION: Native to the Mediterranean region. Double, fragrant, 3-inch (7.5cm) fringed flowers appear midsummer on bushy plants. Leaves are long, slender, grasslike, green.

HEIGHT: 2 to 3 feet (.6 to .9m).

COLOR: Red, pink, yellow, white, mahogany, purple, bicolors.

HARDINESS: Moderately hardy annual; killed by severe frost.

CULTURE: Prefers full sun, sandy or well-drained loam soil, cool nights. Best grown from seed started indoors 8 weeks before outdoor planting. Tall varieties may need staking.

USES: Beds, borders, cutting.

DIANTHUS CHINENSIS

COMMON NAME: Rainbow pinks

FAMILY: Caryophyllaceaea (Carnations)

DESCRIPTION: Native to Europe and Asia. Mound-shaped plants with grasslike blue-green leaves are covered with lightly fragrant star-shaped flowers in spring; some varieties have fringed petal tips.

HEIGHT: 18 inches (46cm).

COLOR: White, pink, red, mahogany, bicolors.

HARDINESS: Though biennial, grows almost anywhere as a hardy annual, if flowering is timed for cool nights. Generally killed by severe freezing weather. Allow 12 weeks from seed to flowering.

CULTURE: Prefers full sun, excellent drainage, cool nights. Start seed indoors 8 weeks before outdoor planting. In mild climates, direct-sow in autumn.

USES: Edging beds and borders, mass plantings, rock gardens, dry walls.

DIASCIA RIGESCENS

COMMON NAME: Twinspur

FAMILY: Scrophulariaceae (Figworts)

DESCRIPTION: Native to South Africa. Plants grow as loose-mounded clumps with thin stems topped by spikes of 1-inch (2.5cm) flowers that have prominent lower lips and dark throats.

HEIGHT: 18 inches (46cm).

COLOR: Pink with deeper pink throats.

HARDINESS: Killed by severe frost. Grows mostly in mild-climate areas since plants cannot tolerate high heat.

CULTURE: Prefers full sun, good drainage, a cool, dry climate. Start seed indoors 7 to 8 weeks before outdoor planting after frost danger.

USES: Edging beds and borders; massed bedding.

DIGITALIS PURPUREA 'FOXY'

COMMON NAME: Common foxglove

FAMILY: Scrophulariaceae (Figworts)

DESCRIPTION: Native to Europe. Tall flower spikes are studded with spotted, tubular florets. Leaves are hairy, heart-shaped, dark green.

HEIGHT: 4 to 5 feet (1.2 to 1.5m).

COLOR: Red, purple, pink, yellow, white.

HARDINESS: Grows almost anywhere as a hardy annual.

CULTURE: Grows in sun or shade. Prefers well-drained loam soil, cool nights. Start seed indoors 8 to 10 weeks before outdoor planting. May need staking.

USES: Beds, borders, containers, cutting. All parts are poisonous.

DIMORPHOTHECA SINUATA

COMMON NAME: Cape marigold; African daisies

FAMILY: Compositae (Daisies)

DESCRIPTION: Native to South Africa. Low-spreading plants produce masses of shimmering daisylike flowers up to 2 inches (5cm) across. Leaves are small, narrow, toothed.

HEIGHT: 12 inches (31cm).

COLOR: Yellow, orange, white, pink with black eyes.

HARDINESS: Killed by severe frost. Grows almost anywhere but flowers best where summers are cool.

CULTURE: Prefers full sun, sandy or well-drained loam soil, cool nights. Direct-sow seeds after frost danger in spring.

USES: Beds, borders, containers, massing.

DOLICHOS LABLAB

COMMON NAME: Hyacinth bean

FAMILY: Leguminosae (Peas)

DESCRIPTION: Native to Egypt. Decorative, fast-growing vine with heart-shaped bronze leaves produces attractive pealike flowers and decorative seed pods.

HEIGHT: 10 feet (3m).

COLOR: Purple flowers in clusters, shiny purple pods.

HARDINESS: Grows almost anywhere as a tender annual.

CULTURE: Prefers full sun and fertile loam soil with good drainage. Direct-sow after frost danger, planting seeds 1 inch (2.5cm) deep, 12 inches apart in full sun.

USES: Decorating arbors, trellises, chain link fences.

DOROTHEANTHUS BELLIDIFORMIS

COMMON NAME: Livingstone daisy

FAMILY: Aizoaceae (Ice plants)

DESCRIPTION: Native to South Africa. Daisylike flowers in iridescent colors are borne on low-spreading plants during cool weather. Leaves are small, smooth, succulent.

HEIGHT: 6 inches (15cm).

COLOR: Red, pink, purple, white, yellow, orange, bicolors.

HARDINESS: Killed by severe frost. Grows well only in areas with cool summers.

CULTURE: Demands full sun, sandy or well-drained loam soil, cool nights. Best grown from seed, direct-sown.

USES: Beds, borders, edging, massing, containers.

DYSSODIA TENUILOBA

COMMON NAME: Dahlberg daisy

FAMILY: Compositae (Daisies)

DESCRIPTION: Native to Mexico. Yellow daisylike ½-inch (13mm) flowers bloom all summer on low-spreading plants. Leaves are fine, needlelike, bright green.

HEIGHT: 6 inches (15cm).

COLOR: Canary yellow.

HARDINESS: Killed by frost. Grows almost anywhere as a tender annual.

CULTURE: Prefers full sun, sandy or well-drained loam soil. Tolerates high heat. Direct-sow seed after frost danger in spring.

USES: Edging beds and borders, temporary ground cover, containers.

EMILIA JAVANICA

COMMON NAME: Flora's paintbrush; tassel flower

FAMILY: Compositae (Daisies)

DESCRIPTION: Native to the tropics. Thistlelike flowers about ½ inch (13mm) across are borne on long, wiry stems. Leaves are slender, lancelike. Early summer-flowering.

HEIGHT: 2 feet (.6m).

COLOR: Reddish orange, yellow.

HARDINESS: Killed by frost. Grows almost anywhere as a tender annual.

CULTURE: Prefers full sun, good drainage; tolerates impoverished soil. Best grown from seed, direct-sown after frost danger. Tolerates crowding.

USES: Mostly grown in cutting gardens and mixed into perennial gardens.

ERYSIMUM HIERACIIFOLIUM

COMMON NAME: Siberian wallflower

FAMILY: Cruciferae (Cabbages)

DESCRIPTION: Native to central and eastern Europe. Wallflowerlike flowers are mostly four-petaled; borne on an erect spike during cool nights in early summer. Leaves are slender, dark green.

HEIGHT: Up to 3½ feet (1.1m).

COLOR: Yellow, orange.

HARDINESS: Grows almost anywhere as a hardy biennial when nights are cool.

CULTURE: Prefers full sun, well-drained sandy or loam soil, cool nights. Best grown from seed started indoors 8 to 10 weeks before outdoor planting.

USES: Beds, borders, meadow gardens, cutting.

ESCHSCHOLZIA CALIFORNICA

COMMON NAME: California poppy

FAMILY: Papaveraceae (Poppies)

DESCRIPTION: Native to California. Shimmering four-petaled or semidouble flowers grow up to 3 inches (7.5cm) across; bloom when nights are cool. Feathery, gray-green foliage creates a bushy plant.

HEIGHT: 12 inches (31cm).

COLOR: Orange, yellow, pink, red, white.

HARDINESS: Hardy annual killed by severe frost. Grows almost anywhere as a cool-season annual.

CULTURE: Prefers full sun, sandy or well-drained loam soil, cool nights. Best grown from seed, direct-sown.

USES: Beds, borders, rock gardens, meadow gardens.

EUPHORBIA MARGINATA

COMMON NAME: Snow-on-the-mountain

FAMILY: Euphorbiaceae (Euphorbias)

DESCRIPTION: Native to North America. Plants grow bushy and erect with silvery green foliage and young leaf whorls trimmed with pure white. Tiny white flowers are clustered inside each leaf whorl.

HEIGHT: 2 to 3 feet (.6 to .9m).

COLOR: Snow white.

HARDINESS: Killed by frost. Grows almost anywhere as a tender annual.

CULTURE: Prefers full sun, sandy or well-drained loam soil. Best grown from seed, direct-sown.

USES: Mixed beds and borders. Be aware that milky sap from cut stems can cause skin irritation.

EUSTOMA GRANDIFLORUM (also LISIANTHUS RUSSELLIANUS)

COMMON NAME: Prairie gentian

FAMILY: Gentianaceae (Gentians)

DESCRIPTION: Native to Texas. Cup-shaped flowers are held erect in clusters on slender stems. Leaves are spear-shaped, blue-green.

HEIGHT: 3 feet (.9m).

COLOR: Blue, pink, white with dark centers.

HARDINESS: Killed by frost. Grows almost anywhere as a tender annual.

CULTURE: Prefers full sun, sandy or well-drained loam soil. Best grown from seed started indoors 8 weeks before outdoor planting. Generally needs staking.

USES: Beds, borders, cutting.

FELICIA AMELLOIDES

COMMON NAME: Kingfisher daisy

FAMILY: Compositae (Daisies)

DESCRIPTION: Native to South Africa. Cheerful, sky blue, daisylike flowers, 1 inch (2.5cm) across, grow on low, spreading plants. Leaves are dainty, indented, bright green.

HEIGHT: 9 inches (23cm).

COLOR: Blue with yellow centers.

HARDINESS: Killed by frost. Grows almost anywhere as a tender annual.

CULTURE: Prefers full sun, sandy or well-drained loam soil, cool nights. Best grown from seed, direct-sown.

USES: Edging, dry walls, rock gardens, containers.

FRAGARIA VESCA

COMMON NAME: Woodland strawberry; fraises des bois.

FAMILY: Rosaceae (Roses)

DESCRIPTION: Native to cold-winter regions. The true species has been used as an ornamental for centuries. New hybrids such as 'Sweetheart' have larger flowers and day-neutral tendencies (the ability to flower and set fruit continuously all season). Plants are low-growing, mounded, compact, with serrated oval leaves arranged in trios. Star-shaped flowers appearing in spring are most prolific when nights are cool.

HEIGHT: 12 inches (31cm).

COLOR: White flowers, red fruit.

HARDINESS: Grows almost anywhere as a hardy annual; survives freezing winters to grow as a perennial.

CULTURE: Prefers full sun, good drainage, fertile loam soil. Start seed indoors 8 weeks before outdoor planting.

USES: Edging, ground cover.

GAILLARDIA PULCHELLA

COMMON NAME: Blanket flower

FAMILY: Compositae (Daisies)

DESCRIPTION: Native to North America. Covered in summer with double and single 2½-inch (6.5cm) flowers. Leaves are narrow, toothed, dark green.

HEIGHT: 2 to 3 feet (.6 to .9m).

COLOR: Yellow, orange, red, bicolors.

HARDINESS: Killed by severe frost. Grows almost anywhere as a tender annual.

CULTURE: Prefers full sun, sandy or well-drained loam soil. Best grown from seed, direct-sown.

USES: Beds, borders, cutting, meadow gardens.

GAZANIA RIGENS

COMMON NAME: Treasure flower

FAMILY: Compositae (Daisies)

DESCRIPTION: Native to South Africa. Shimmering, daisylike flowers up to 4 inches (10cm) across bloom on low, spreading plants. Flowers stay closed on cloudy days. Leaves are lancelike, gray-green.

HEIGHT: 12 inches (31cm).

COLOR: Yellow, red, orange; black zone around petal center.

HARDINESS: Killed by frost. Grows almost anywhere as a tender annual.

CULTURE: Demands full sun, sandy or well-drained loam soil, cool nights. Best grown from seed, direct-sown.

USES: Mixed beds and borders.

GERBERA JAMESONII

COMMON NAME: Transvaal daisy, gerbera daisy

FAMILY: Compositae (Daisies)

DESCRIPTION: Native to South Africa. Plants form rosettes of broad, toothed, shiny, dark green leaves and erect stems topped with daisylike flowers up to 4 inches (10cm) across.

HEIGHT: To 18 inches (46cm).

COLOR: White, yellow, red, pink, orange.

HARDINESS: Tender perennial, killed by frost. Best grown as a tender annual to flower during cool weather. May overwinter in zones 8 to 10.

CULTURE: Prefers full sun, fertile, sandy or well-drained loam soil. Start seed indoors 10 weeks before outdoor planting.

USES: Massing in beds and borders. Sensational flowering pot plant raised under glass.

GILIA CAPITATA

COMMON NAME: Queen-Anne's-thimble

FAMILY: Polemoniaceae (Phlox)

DESCRIPTION: Native to California. Sprawling plants with finely cut leaves bear cloverlike, ¾-inch (19mm), rounded flower heads. Flowers continuously through summer months.

HEIGHT: Up to 2½ feet (.8m).

COLOR: Blue.

HARDINESS: Tolerates mild frost. Grows almost anywhere as a hardy annual.

CULTURE: Prefers full sun, sandy or loam soil. Direct-sow, covering seeds just enough to anchor them. Tolerates crowding.

USES: Mostly used as an edging so it can sprawl into paths and as a dainty cut flower.

GOMPHRENA GLOBOSA

COMMON NAME: Globe amaranth

FAMILY: Amaranthaceae (Amaranthus)

DESCRIPTION: Native to India. Papery, cloverlike, globular flowers are produced continuously all summer on bushy, billowing plants. Leaves are slender, pointed.

HEIGHT: 2 to 3 feet (.6 to .9m).

COLOR: Magenta, pink, white, orange.

HARDINESS: Killed by frost. Grows almost anywhere as a tender annual.

CULTURE: Prefers full sun, sandy or well-drained loam soil. Popular where summers are warm and sunny. Highly heat- and drought-tolerant. Best grown from seed, direct-sown.

USES: Beds, borders, cutting. Popular for drying.

GOMPHRENA HAAGEANA AUREA

COMMON NAME: Orange globe amaranth

FAMILY: Amaranthaceae (Amaranthus)

DESCRIPTION: Native to Texas. Cloverlike flowers have papery petals and grow on mounded plants. Summer-flowering leaves are slender, lancelike, dark green.

HEIGHT: 2½ feet (.8m).

COLOR: Orange, red.

HARDINESS: Grows almost anywhere as a tender annual. Perennial in frost-free climates.

CULTURE: Tolerates high heat and drought. Seed can be direct-sown or started indoors 6 weeks before outdoor planting. Needs full sun, good drainage.

USES: Mixed beds and borders. Good for cutting and dried flower arrangements.

GYPSOPHILA ELEGANS

COMMON NAME: Baby's-breath

FAMILY: Caryophyllaceae (Carnations)

DESCRIPTION: Native to Europe. Billowing plants are covered in ½-inch (13mm) flowers. Stems and leaves are delicate, wispy, almost completely hidden when plant is in full bloom.

HEIGHT: 2 to 3 feet (.6 to .9m).

COLOR: White, pale pink.

HARDINESS: Killed by frost. Grows almost anywhere as a tender annual.

CULTURE: Prefers full sun, sandy or well-drained loam soil. Best grown from seed, direct-sown.

USES: Mixed beds and borders, cutting.

HELIANTHUS ANNUUS

COMMON NAME: Common sunflower

FAMILY: Compositae (Daisies)

DESCRIPTION: Native to North America. Immense daisylike flowers measure up to 24 inches (61cm) across on tall stems with large, smooth, heart-shaped leaves.

HEIGHT: 8 feet (2.4m).

COLOR: Yellow, orange, mahogany, bicolors.

HARDINESS: Killed by frost. Grows almost anywhere as a tender annual.

CULTURE: Demands full sun, well-drained loam soil. Best grown from seed, direct-sown.

USES: Tall backgrounds for beds and borders.

HELIANTHUS ANNUUS 'TEDDY BEAR'

COMMON NAME: Van Gogh sunflower

FAMILY: Compositae (Daisies)

DESCRIPTION: Native to North America. A dwarf, bushy form of the annual sunflower. Produces rounded double flowers up to 10 inches (25cm) across, resembling sunflowers the artist Van Gogh loved to paint.

HEIGHT: 3 feet (.9m).

COLOR: Golden yellow.

HARDINESS: Killed by frost. Grows almost anywhere as a tender annual.

CULTURE: Prefers full sun, loam soil. Direct-sow seeds 1 inch (2.5cm) deep, 2 feet (.6m) apart. Tolerates high heat and humidity. Grows best where summers are warm and sunny.

USES: Beds, borders, containers, cutting. Seeds attract birds.

HELIANTHUS INTERMEDIUS

COMMON NAME: Hybrid sunflower

FAMILY: Compositae (Daisies)

DESCRIPTION: By crossing the giant sunflower (*H. annuus*) with the cucumber-leaf sunflower (*H. debilis*), breeders have produced a number of branching types with masses of daisylike flowers up to 5 inches (13cm) wide, a wide color range, and a continuous flowering habit. Leaves are heart-shaped, dark green. Summer- and autumn-flowering.

HEIGHT: 5 to 7 feet (1.5 to 2.1m)

COLOR: Yellow, bronze, orange, red, mahogany (some bicolored).

HARDINESS: Killed by frost. Grows almost anywhere as a tender annual.

CULTURE: Needs full sun; not fussy about soil. Direct-sow.

USES: Tall backgrounds, cutting. The seeds are relished by birds.

HELICHRYSUM BRACTEATUM

COMMON NAME: Strawflower

FAMILY: Compositae (Daisies)

DESCRIPTION: Native to Australia. Papery double flowers with pointed petals bloom all summer on upright, bushy plants. Leaves are slender, indented, green.

HEIGHT: 2 to 4 feet (.6 to 1.2m).

COLOR: Red, pink, yellow, orange, white.

HARDINESS: Killed by severe frost. Grows almost anywhere as a tender annual.

CULTURE: Prefers full sun, sandy or well-drained loam soil. Best grown from seed, direct-sown.

USES: Beds, borders. Dwarf types suitable for containers. Popular for drying.

HELIOTROPIUM ARBORESCENS

COMMON NAME: Heliotrope

FAMILY: Boraginaceae (Borages)

DESCRIPTION: Native to Peru. Plants grow erect, with long, broad, textured, dark green leaves that display a bronze cast. Clusters of small fragrant flowers crowd the top of each plant.

HEIGHT: 2 to 3 feet (.6 to .9m).

COLOR: Mainly purple.

HARDINESS: Tender perennial killed by frost; grows almost anywhere as a tender annual.

CULTURE: Prefers full sun, fertile soil. Start seed indoors 10 weeks before outdoor planting.

USES: Mixed beds and borders. Popular greenhouse pot plant for winter color and heavenly vanilla scent.

HELIPTERUM ROSEUM

COMMON NAME: Everlasting; Acroclinium; Rhodanthe

FAMILY: Compositae (Daisies)

DESCRIPTION: Native to the Mediterranean region. Papery, double, daisylike flowers occur in summer on upright plants. Leaves are slender, indented, dark green.

HEIGHT: 3 feet (.9m).

COLOR: Red, pink, white.

HARDINESS: Killed by frost. Grows almost anywhere as a tender annual.

CULTURE: Prefers full sun, sandy or well-drained loam soil, cool nights. Best grown from seed, direct-sown.

USES: Beds, borders. Popular for drying.

HESPERIS MATRONALIS

COMMON NAME: Dame's rocket

FAMILY: Cruciferae (Cabbages)

DESCRIPTION: Native to Europe; naturalized throughout North America. Looks like a cross between stocks and phlox. Fragrant ½-inch (13mm) flowers are borne in clusters at the top of a stiff flowering stem. Leaves are spear-shaped.

HEIGHT: 3 feet (.9m).

COLOR: Pink, lilac, white.

HARDINESS: Hardy biennial that will flower the first season from seed started early indoors.

CULTURE: Prefers full sun or light shade, good drainage. Seed should be direct-sown, pressed into the soil surface as it needs light to germinate. Flowers in early summer when nights are cool.

USES: Mostly grown for cutting and for use in wildflower meadows.

HIBISCUS MOSCHEUTOS

COMMON NAME: Hardy hibiscus; swamp mallow; rose mallow

FAMILY: Malvaceae (Mallows)

DESCRIPTION: Native to the southeastern United States. Perennial plants of hybrid cultivars will bloom the first season. Upright plants produce incredibly large flowers—up to 10 inches (25cm) across. Leaves are heart-shaped, light green.

HEIGHT: 4 to 5 feet (1.2 to 1.5m).

COLOR: Red, pink, white, many with dark "eyes."

HARDINESS: Tops are killed by frost. Grows almost anywhere as a tender annual. Roots may overwinter to bloom the following season even in areas with severe winters. Flowers best where summers are warm and sunny.

CULTURE: Prefers full sun, high heat, moist loam soil. Best grown from seed started indoors 6 to 8 weeks before outdoor planting. Soak seeds overnight to aid germination.

USES: Beds, borders, poolside.

HUMULUS JAPONICUS

COMMON NAME: Japanese hop

FAMILY: Cannabaceae (Hemps)

DESCRIPTION: Native to Japan. Grows vigorous, ivylike vines with indented leaves and papery, green oval fruit clusters that turn brown in autumn.

HEIGHT: Up to 10 feet (3m).

COLOR: Green, grown mostly for its ornamental foliage. There is a white and green variegated variety.

HARDINESS: Tolerates mild frost. Grows almost anywhere as a hardy annual.

CULTURE: Prefers full sun, sandy or loam soil. Direct-sow in early spring. Needs strong support, such as a trellis.

USES: Mostly used to cover chain link fences and arbors. Popular ornamental in herb gardens.

HUNNEMANNIA FUMARIIFOLIA

COMMON NAME: Mexican tulip poppy

FAMILY: Papaveraceae (Poppies)

DESCRIPTION: Native to Mexico. Upright plants produce shimmering, poppylike flowers in summer. Leaves are deeply indented, gray-green.

HEIGHT: 2 feet (.6m).

COLOR: Canary yellow.

HARDINESS: Killed by frost. Grows almost anywhere as a tender annual.

CULTURE: Prefers full sun, sandy or well-drained loam soil. Drought-resistant. Best grown from seed, direct-sown.

USES: Beds, borders, meadow gardens.

IBERIS UMBELLATA

COMMON NAME: Candytuft

FAMILY: Cruciferae (Cabbages)

DESCRIPTION: Native to Spain. Low, spreading plants bear 3-inch (7.5cm) flower clusters. Leaves are narrow, pointed, dark green.

HEIGHT: 12 inches (31cm).

COLOR: Red, pink, purple, white.

HARDINESS: Grows almost anywhere as a hardy annual.

CULTURE: Prefers full sun, sandy or well-drained soil, cool nights. Grown best from seed, direct-sown.

USES: Edging beds and borders.

IMPATIENS BALSAMINA

COMMON NAME: Balsam

FAMILY: Balsaminaceae (Balsams)

DESCRIPTION: Native to India. Erect plants produce camellialike flowers along succulent stems. Leaves are spear-shaped, serrated.

HEIGHT: 2 feet (.6m).

COLOR: Red, pink, purple, white, bicolors.

HARDINESS: Killed by frost. Grows almost anywhere as a tender annual.

CULTURE: Grows in sun or shade. Prefers cool, moist, humus-rich soil. Best grown from seed started indoors 6 to 8 weeks before outdoor planting.

USES: Beds, borders.

IMPATIENS WALLERANA

COMMON NAME: Patience plant

FAMILY: Balsaminaceae (Balsams)

DESCRIPTION: Native to South America. Mostly four-petaled, 2- to 3-inch (5 to 7.5cm) flowers bloom continuously on mounded, spreading, succulent plants. Leaves are pointed, serrated.

HEIGHT: 1 to 2 feet (.3 to .6m).

COLOR: Red, white, purple, pink, bicolors.

HARDINESS: Killed by frost. Grows almost anywhere as a tender annual.

CULTURE: Prefers light shade, cool, moist, humus-rich soil. Best grown from seed started indoors 8 to 10 weeks before outdoor planting.

USES: Beds, borders, window boxes, hanging baskets, other containers.

IMPOMOEA ALBA

COMMON NAME: Moonflower

FAMILY: Convolvulaeae (Morning-glories)

DESCRIPTION: Native to South America. Rounded flowers bloom at night and in early morning in summer on vigorous vines with heart-shaped leaves.

HEIGHT: 10 feet (3m).

COLOR: White.

HARDINESS: Killed by frost. Grows almost anywhere as a tender annual.

CULTURE: Prefers full sun, sandy or well-drained loam soil. Best grown from seed, direct-sown; soak overnight to aid germination. Needs support.

USES: Vine for covering trellises.

IPOMOEA QUAMOCLIT

COMMON NAME: Cypress vine

FAMILY: Convolvulaceae (Morning-glories)

DESCRIPTION: Native to South America. Plants grow into vigorous vines with light green leaves resembling those of the evergreen cypress and 1½-inch (4cm), star-shaped flowers.

HEIGHT: 10 to 20 feet (3 to 6m).

COLOR: Red, white, pink.

HARDINESS: Killed by frost. Grows almost anywhere as a tender annual.

CULTURE: Prefers full sun, moist soil. Start seeds indoors 6 weeks before outdoor planting, soaking first in lukewarm water overnight to aid germination.

USES: Decorating trellises, arbors, fences.

IPOMOEA TRICOLOR

COMMON NAME: Morning-glory

FAMILY: Convolvulaceae (Morning-glories)

DESCRIPTION: Native to Central America. Circular flowers up to 4 inches (10cm) across are produced freely on vigorous, fast-growing vines with bright green, heart-shaped leaves.

HEIGHT: 10 feet (3m).

COLOR: Blue, red, pink, purple, white.

HARDINESS: Killed by frost. Grows almost anywhere as a tender annual.

CULTURE: Prefers full sun, sandy or well-drained loam soil. Flowers close in late afternoon and on cloudy days. Best grown from seed soaked overnight to aid germination, and direct-sown. Needs a trellis for support.

USES: Vine for tall backgrounds and screening.

KOCHIA SCOPARIA

COMMON NAME: Burning bush

FAMILY: Chenopodiaceae (Goosefoots)

DESCRIPTION: Native to Mexico. Bushy plants resemble the evergreen cypress. Bright green leaves turn red in autumn. Flowers are inconspicuous.

HEIGHT: 3 feet (.9m).

COLOR: Grown for its feathery green leaves.

HARDINESS: Killed by frost. Grows almost anywhere as a tender annual.

CULTURE: Prefers full sun, sandy or well-drained loam soil. Drought-tolerant. Best grown from seed started indoors 4 to 6 weeks before outdoor planting.

USES: Background for beds and borders.

LAGURUS OVATUS

COMMON NAME: Hare's-tail

FAMILY: Gramineae (Grasses)

DESCRIPTION: Native to the Mediterranean region. Plants form spiky clumps that bear masses of erect fluffy flower heads ½ inch (13mm) wide, 1 inch (2.5cm) long.

HEIGHT: 2 feet (.6m).

COLOR: White.

HARDINESS: Killed by severe frost. Grows almost anywhere as a moderately hardy annual.

CULTURE: Tolerates poor soil, high heat, humidity. Start seed indoors 8 weeks before outdoor planting in a sunny location.

USES: Good highlight for mixed beds and borders. Flower stems are valued for floral arrangements.

LANTANA CAMARA HYBRIDS

COMMON NAME: Yellow sage

FAMILY: Verbenaceae (Verbenas)

DESCRIPTION: Native to the West Indies. Lancelike leaves crowd woody stems; massed all summer with 2-inch (5cm) circular flower clusters. Spreading plants will trail on the ground and can be trained to climb.

HEIGHT: Up to 3 feet (.9m) in one season.

COLOR: Yellow, orange, white, red, pink, bicolors.

HARDINESS: Killed by frost. Grows almost anywhere as a tender annual. Perennial in frost-free areas.

CULTURE: Prefers full sun, sandy or loam soil with good drainage. Start seed early indoors, and set 10-week-old transplants outdoors after frost danger. Can be propagated from cuttings.

USES: Massing in beds and borders, ground cover, hanging baskets, containers. Also makes a good flowering house plant.

LATHYRUS ODORATUS

COMMON NAME: Sweet pea

FAMILY: Leguminosae (Peas)

DESCRIPTION: Native to Sicily. Pealike flowers are fragrant, cluster on wiry stems. Leaves are cloverlike, blue-green. Stems have tendrils for climbing.

HEIGHT: 2 to 5 feet (.6 to 1.5m).

COLOR: Red, white, blue, pink.

HARDINESS: Hardy annual; tolerates mild frosts. Grows almost anywhere as a cool-season annual.

CULTURE: Prefers full sun, cool, moist soil. Best grown from seed, direct-sown. Needs cool nights to bloom. Tall varieties need staking.

USES: Beds, borders, cutting.

LAVANDULA ANGUSTIFOLIA 'LAVENDER LADY'

COMMON NAME: Annual English lavender

FAMILY: Labiatae (Mint)

DESCRIPTION: Native to the Mediterranean region. Features cushionlike clumps of slender flower spikes and spear-shaped, gray-green leaves. 'Lavender Lady' is a special perennial lavender that will flower the first year from seed. Entire plant is fragrant. Summer- and autumn-flowering until frost.

HEIGHT: 12 to 18 inches (31 to 46cm).

COLOR: Blue.

HARDINESS: Moderately hardy perennial best grown as a tender annual. Top growth dies after frost, but plants may survive mild winters to bloom again as perennials.

CULTURE: Grows in sun or light shade; prefers a sandy, well-drained soil. Start seed indoors 8 weeks before outdoor planting after frost danger.

USES: Massing in beds and borders. Beautiful for edging paths and cutting.

LAVATERA TRIMESTRIS

COMMON NAME: Rose mallow; tree mallow

FAMILY: Malvaceae (Mallows)

DESCRIPTION: Native to the Mediterranean region. Bushy plants produce masses of hibiscuslike flowers that shimmer like satin. Flowers are on erect stems with spear-shaped, serrated, dark green leaves.

HEIGHT: 3 to 4 feet (.9 to 1.2m).

COLOR: Pink, white.

HARDINESS: Grows almost anywhere as a hardy annual.

CULTURE: Prefers full sun, sandy or well-drained loam soil. Best grown from seed, direct-sown.

USES: Beds, borders.

LAYIA PLATYGLOSSA

COMMON NAME: Tidy-tips

FAMILY: Compositae (Daisies)

DESCRIPTION: Native to California. Daisylike 2-inch (5cm) flowers are held erect on stiff stems; leaves are slender and narrow; petals are attractively fringed.

HEIGHT: 12 inches (31cm).

COLOR: Yellow with white tips.

HARDINESS: Hardy annual that grows best where summers are cool.

CULTURE: Prefers full sun, good drainage, cool nights. Direct-sow.

USES: Mixed beds and borders, wildflower meadows.

LIMNANTHES DOUGLASII

COMMON NAME: Meadow foam; scrambled eggs

FAMILY: Limnanthaceae (Meadow foams)

DESCRIPTION: Native to California. Shimmering, five-petaled, 1-inch (2.5cm) flowers bloom briefly in early summer on low, spreading plants. Leaves are delicate, indented, green.

HEIGHT: 6 inches (15cm).

COLOR: Yellow with white petal tips.

HARDINESS: Killed by severe frost. Grows almost anywhere as a moderately hardy annual to flower during cool weather.

CULTURE: Prefers full sun, moist loam soil, cool nights. Best grown from seed, direct-sown.

USES: Edging beds and borders, massing, meadow gardens.

LIMONIUM SINUATUM

COMMON NAME: Statice

FAMILY: Plumbaginaceae (Leadworts)

DESCRIPTION: Native to the Mediterranean region. Upright, bushy plants have wiry stems bearing dense, papery flower clusters. Leaves are narrow, lancelike, dark green.

HEIGHT: 2 to 3 feet (.6 to .9m).

COLOR: Purple, blue, pink, yellow, white.

HARDINESS: Killed by frost. Grows almost anywhere as a tender annual.

CULTURE: Prefers full sun, sandy or well-drained loam soil, cool nights. Best grown from seed, direct-sown.

USES: Beds, borders, cutting. Popular for drying.

LINARIA MAROCCANA

COMMON NAME: Toadflax

FAMILY: Scrophulariaceae (Figworts)

DESCRIPTION: Native to Morocco. Snapdragonlike flowers are held erect on wiry stems. Leaves are narrow, grasslike.

HEIGHT: 12 inches (31cm).

COLOR: Red, orange, yellow, purple, white, bicolors.

HARDINESS: Hardy annual. Grows almost anywhere to flower during cool weather.

CULTURE: Prefers full sun, sandy or well-drained loam soil, cool nights. Best grown from seed, direct-sown. Tolerates crowding.

USES: Generally planted as drifts of color in beds and borders. Good for cutting.

LINUM GRANDIFLORUM

COMMON NAME: Scarlet flax

FAMILY: Linaceae (Flaxes)

DESCRIPTION: Native to North Africa. Plants are slender and wiry with narrow, pointed leaves topped by cup-shaped, 1-inch (2.5cm) flowers.

HEIGHT: 12 to 18 inches (31 to 46cm).

COLOR: Scarlet.

HARDINESS: Will grow almost anywhere as a hardy annual if flowering is timed for cool weather 6 to 8 weeks after sowing.

CULTURE: Prefers full sun, good drainage; tolerates poor, sandy soil. Direct-sow. Flowers best when nights are cool. Tolerates crowding.

USES: Mixed beds and borders, wildflower meadows.

LOBELIA ERINUS

COMMON NAME: Edging lobelia

FAMILY: Lobeliaceae (Lobelias)

DESCRIPTION: Native to South Africa. Mounded, spreading plants are covered with ¼-inch (6mm) orchidlike flowers. Slender stems will cascade over pots and hanging baskets. Leaves are small, toothed.

HEIGHT: 6 inches (15cm).

COLOR: Blue, red, pink, white.

HARDINESS: Hardy annual. Grows almost anywhere if plantings timed to flower during cool nights.

CULTURE: Prefers full sun, sandy or well-drained loam soil, cool nights. Best grown from seed started indoors 10 weeks before outdoor planting.

USES: Edging beds and borders, hanging baskets, window boxes, other containers.

LOBULARIA MARITIMA

COMMON NAME: Sweet alyssum

FAMILY: Cruciferae (Cabbages)

DESCRIPTION: Native to the Mediterranean region. Clusters of tiny fragrant flowers are produced all summer on low, spreading plants composed of fine green leaves.

HEIGHT: 6 inches (15cm).

COLOR: White, pink, deep blue.

HARDINESS: Grows almost anywhere as a hardy annual. Self-seeds readily.

CULTURE: Prefers full sun, sandy or well-drained loam soil, cool nights. Best grown from seed, direct-sown.

USES: Temporary ground cover, edging beds and borders, decorating cracks between flagstone; also windowboxes, hanging baskets, other container plantings.

LONAS ANNUA (also *L. INODORA*)

COMMON NAME: Yellow ageratum

FAMILY: Compositae (Daisies)

DESCRIPTION: Native to Africa. Clusters of buttonlike, ½-inch (13mm) flowers are held erect on aromatic, stiff stems. Leaves are toothed.

HEIGHT: 12 inches (31cm).

COLOR: Golden yellow.

HARDINESS: Killed by frost. Grows almost anywhere as a tender annual, though flowers best when nights are cool.

CULTURE: Prefers full sun, good drainage, cool nights. Direct-sow into garden soil. Flowers within 8 weeks.

USES: Mostly grown for cutting.

LUPINUS TEXENSIS

COMMON NAME: Texas bluebonnet

FAMILY: Leguminosae (Peas)

DESCRIPTION: Native to Texas. Erect flower spikes are surrounded by whorls of five leaflets. Flowers are pealike.

HEIGHT: 12 inches (31cm).

COLOR: Blue, sometimes white.

HARDINESS: Hardy annual that requires cool nights to bloom well. Does best in zones 8 to 10.

CULTURE: Requires full sun and cool nights. Prefers to grow from seed, direct-sown into alkaline soil.

USES: Mass plantings, especially in meadows where plants may reseed and naturalize, providing seed pods are allowed to ripen before cutting.

LYNCHIS COELI-ROSA (also *SILENE COELI-ROSA*)

COMMON NAME: Rose-of-heaven; viscaria

FAMILY: Caryophyllaceae (Carnations)

DESCRIPTION: Native to Russia. Possesses delicate stems and narrow, pointed leaves; the branching plants are covered with masses of 1-inch (2.5cm), star-shaped flowers.

HEIGHT: Up to 12 inches (31cm).

COLOR: White, red, pink, blue.

HARDINESS: Moderately hardy, tolerates mild frosts. Grows almost anywhere as an annual if plantings timed to flower when nights are cool.

CULTURE: Prefers sandy, well-drained soil; blooms in summer when nights are cool. Direct-sow in early spring, covering seeds just enough to anchor them. Tolerates crowding.

USES: Massing in mixed beds and borders. Popular choice for coastal gardens.

MACHAERANTHERA TANACETIFOLIA

COMMON NAME: Tahoka daisy

FAMILY: Compositae (Daisies)

DESCRIPTION: Native to Texas. Asterlike flowers are borne on slender stems with narrow, toothed leaves.

HEIGHT: 18 inches (46cm).

COLOR: Lavender-blue with yellow centers.

HARDINESS: Killed by frost. Grows almost anywhere as a tender annual, but flowers best when nights are cool.

CULTURE: Prefers full sun, good drainage. Direct-sow or start seed indoors 8 weeks before outdoor planting where summers get hot. Direct-sow in autumn for extra-early spring blooms in mild-winter climates.

USES: Mixed beds and borders, cutting.

MALCOLMIA MARITIMA

COMMON NAME: Virginia stock

FAMILY: Cruciferae (Cabbages)

DESCRIPTION: Native to the Mediterranean region. Branching, compact plants have delicate stems, narrow leaves, and masses of small four-petaled, fragrant, phloxlike flowers.

HEIGHT: 12 inches (31cm).

COLOR: White, rosy red, purple, pink.

HARDINESS: Will grow almost anywhere as a hardy annual if flowering is timed for cool weather (8 to 10 weeks after sowing).

CULTURE: Prefers full sun or light shade, good drainage. Direct-sow in garden soil; sow in autumn for extra-early blooms in mild-climate areas. Readily self-seeds in coastal gardens.

USES: Mixed beds and borders.

MATTHIOLA INCANA

COMMON NAME: Brompton stock

FAMILY: Cruciferae (Cabbages)

DESCRIPTION: Native to southern Europe. Plants form erect flower spikes with long, tonguelike leaves and mostly double, fragrant, 1½-inch (4cm) flowers clustered at the top.

HEIGHT: 2 to 3 feet (.6 to .9m).

COLOR: Red, white, lavender-blue, yellow.

HARDINESS: Hardy annual that is grown mostly in mild-winter areas for spring flowering while conditions are cool.

CULTURE: Prefers full sun, good drainage, sandy garden soil, cool days and nights. Best grown from seed, direct-sown in autumn for early spring flowering or started indoors 8 weeks before outdoor planting. Flower buds will not form when temperature exceeds 72°F (22.2°C).

USES: Mixed beds and borders, backgrounds, cutting.

MATTHIOLA LONGIPETALA BICORNIS

COMMON NAME: Evening stock

FAMILY: Cruciferae (Cabbages)

DESCRIPTION: Native to Europe. Plants grow delicate, upright stems with slender, pointed leaves. Masses of star-shaped, four-petaled, highly fragrant flowers open at dusk.

HEIGHT: 2 feet (.6m).

COLOR: White, pink, purple.

HARDINESS: Hardy annual that flowers best during cool nights.

CULTURE: Prefers full sun, good drainage, sandy garden soil, cool days and nights. Direct-sow. In mild-climate areas, sow in autumn for extra-early spring flowering. Tolerates crowding.

USES: Mixed beds and borders, fragrance gardens.

MELAMPODIUM PALUDOSUM

COMMON NAME: Cushion zinnia

FAMILY: Compositae (Daisies)

DESCRIPTION: Native to Mexico. Dense, mound-shaped plants possess smooth, pointed leaves and become covered with 1-inch (2.5cm) daisylike flowers all summer.

HEIGHT: 3 feet (.9m).

COLOR: Yellow.

HARDINESS: Killed by frost. Grows almost anywhere as a tender annual.

CULTURE: Prefers full sun, warm weather, good drainage. Direct-sow after frost danger in spring.

USES: Highlight in beds and borders; temporary hedge.

MENTZELIA LINDLEYI

COMMON NAME: Bartonia

FAMILY: Loasaceae (Bartonias)

DESCRIPTION: Native to California. Grows erect, branching stems with toothed leaves. Flowers are fragrant, poppylike, iridescent, up to 2½ inches (6.5cm) across, and open at night. Summer-flowering.

HEIGHT: Up to 2 feet (.6m).

COLOR: Yellow.

HARDINESS: Tolerates mild frosts. Grows almost anywhere as hardy annual.

CULTURE: Prefers full sun, sandy or loam soil. Direct-sow, thinning to 12 inches (31cm) apart.

USES: Accent in mixed beds and borders. Good for drought-tolerant landscapes.

MIMULUS × HYBRIDUS

COMMON NAME: Monkey flower

FAMILY: Scrophulariaceae (Figworts)

DESCRIPTION: Developed from species native to the northwest coast of North America. Tubular 2½-inch (6.5cm) flowers are exotically spotted, have a prominent lower lip. Heart-shaped, velvety, green leaves form mounded plants. Blooms in early summer during cool weather.

HEIGHT: 9 to 12 inches (23 to 31 cm).

COLOR: Red, orange, yellow, white, usually with red spots.

HARDINESS: Killed by severe frost. Grows almost anywhere as a hardy annual to flower when nights are cool.

CULTURE: Prefers full sun, cool, moist soil, cool nights. Best grown from seed started indoors 10 weeks before outdoor planting.

USES: Beds, borders, edging.

MIRABILIS JALAPA

COMMON NAME: Four-o'clock

FAMILY: Nyctaginaceae (Four-o'clocks)

DESCRIPTION: Native to Japan. Bushy plants grow lancelike, green leaves and 1½-inch (4cm) petunialike flowers that can have several colors in the same flower and also several colors on the same plant. Flowers stay closed until the late afternoon on sunny days, remain open all day on cloudy days.

HEIGHT: To 3 feet (.9m).

COLOR: White, yellow, pink, orange, red, bicolors, tricolors.

HARDINESS: Tender annual, killed by frost. Lives on as a perennial in frost-free areas, especially zone 10.

CULTURE: Prefers full sun, tolerates poor soil providing drainage is good. Start seed indoors 6 weeks before outdoor planting. Plants also develop tubers, which can be lifted and stored indoors for replanting after frost danger.

USES: Good accent in mixed beds and borders. Especially attractive in old-fashioned, cottage-style gardens.

MOLUCCELLA LAEVIS

COMMON NAME: Bells-of-Ireland

FAMILY: Labiatae (Mints)

DESCRIPTION: Native to Syria. Bushy, spreading plants have slender flower spikes composed of outward-facing, bell-shaped bracts, with inconspicuous white flowers at the center of each bract. Leaves are broad, indented, bright green. Summer-flowering.

HEIGHT: 2 feet (.6m).

COLOR: Green bracts.

HARDINESS: Killed by frost. Grows almost anywhere as a tender annual.

CULTURE: Prefers full sun, sandy or well-drained loam soil. Best grown from seed, direct-sown after soaking overnight in lukewarm water to aid germination.

USES: Beds, borders, cutting. Popular for drying.

MONARDA CITRIODORA

COMMON NAME: Lemon beebalm

FAMILY: Labiatae (Mints)

DESCRIPTION: Native to North America. Tubular flowers are arranged in a crown on erect stems. Leaves are spear-shaped, serrated, gray-green. Aroma is suggestive of lemons.

HEIGHT: 3 feet (.9m).

COLOR: Pink.

HARDINESS: Killed by severe frost. Grows almost anywhere as a tender annual. Grows best where summers are warm and sunny.

CULTURE: Prefers full sun and a sandy or well-drained loam soil. Start seed indoors 6 to 8 weeks before outdoor planting, or direct-sow after frost danger.

USES: Massing in beds and borders, especially as a tall background.

MYOSOTIS SYLVATICA

COMMON NAME: Garden forget-me-not

FAMILY: Boraginaceae (Borages)

DESCRIPTION: Native to Europe. Plants form rosettes of tongue-shaped dark green leaves and branching flower stems with clusters of dainty ⅜-inch (9mm), five-petaled flowers.

HEIGHT: 12 inches (31cm).

COLOR: Blue, pink, sometimes white.

HARDINESS: Hardy biennial that can be grown as a hardy annual, with planting timed for flowering during cool weather.

CULTURE: Prefers sun or light shade, moist soil. The variety 'Blue Bird' can be forced to flower in spring by starting seed indoors 10 weeks before outdoor planting. In mild-climate areas, seed can be direct-sown in autumn.

USES: Edging tulip and pansy beds; massing under orchard trees, along stream and pond margins.

NEMESIA STRUMOSA

COMMON NAME: Pouch nemesia

FAMILY: Scrophulariaceae (Figworts)

DESCRIPTION: Native to South Africa. Plants grow erect, square stems with spear-shaped, serrated leaves and clusters of 1-inch (2.5cm) flowers with prominent lower lips.

HEIGHT: 2 feet (.6m).

COLOR: Yellow, white, orange, pink, purple, red.

HARDINESS: Tender annual killed by frost. Suitable for growing only in areas with cool summer temperatures.

CULTURE: Prefers full sun, good drainage, cool days and nights. Start seed indoors 10 weeks before outdoor planting.

USES: Mostly used for massing in beds and borders.

NEMOPHILA MENZIESII

COMMON NAME: Baby-blue-eyes

FAMILY: Hydrophyllaceae (Waterleaves)

DESCRIPTION: Native to California. Delicate-looking plants are low-growing, with leaves composed of small, toothed leaflets. Cup-shaped, 1-inch (2.5cm) flowers.

HEIGHT: 12 inches (31cm).

COLOR: Blue.

HARDINESS: Hardy annual best suited to areas with cool summers.

CULTURE: Prefers full sun or light shade. Direct-sow in garden soil. Autumn sowings in mild-winter areas will ensure extra-early spring flowers.

USES: Edging beds and borders; rock gardens; planting between flagstones.

NICANDRA PHYSALODES

COMMON NAME: Shoo-fly plant

FAMILY: Solanaceae (Nightshades)

DESCRIPTION: Native to South America. Cup-shaped, 1-inch (2.5cm) flowers are followed by yellow, lanternlike seed cases. Leaves are indented, dark green. Slight musky flower fragrance repels many kinds of flying insects.

HEIGHT: 2 feet (.6m).

COLOR: Blue.

HARDINESS: Killed by frost. Grows almost anywhere as a tender annual.

CULTURE: Prefers full sun, sandy or well-drained loam soil. Best grown from seed started indoors 6 weeks before outdoor planting.

USES: Mostly grown as a pot plant.

NICOTIANA ALATA

COMMON NAME: Flowering tobacco

FAMILY: Solanaceae (Nightshades)

DESCRIPTION: Native to South America. Star-shaped, 1-inch (2.5cm) tubular flowers bloom in summer on slender stems above dark green velvety leaves, forming a rosette. Old varieties close up in the afternoon.

HEIGHT: 2 to 4 feet (.6 to 1.2m).

COLOR: Red, pink, white, yellow, lime green, purple.

HARDINESS: Killed by frost. Grows almost anywhere as a tender annual.

CULTURE: Prefers full sun, sandy or well-drained loam soil. Best grown from seed started indoors 6 to 8 weeks before outdoor planting.

USES: Beds, borders, containers.

NICOTIANA SYLVESTRIS

COMMON NAME: Fragrant tobacco

FAMILY: Solanaceae (Nightshades)

DESCRIPTION: Native to South America. Plants grow large, spear-shaped leaves that resemble tobacco and erect, tapering stems topped with clusters of fragrant, tubular flowers. Summer- and autumn-flowering.

HEIGHT: To 6 feet (1.8m).

COLOR: White.

HARDINESS: Tender perennial, mostly grown as a tender annual. Overwinters in zones 9 and 10.

CULTURE: Grows in sun or light shade; prefers fertile, sandy or well-drained loam soil. Best grown from seed started indoors 6 weeks before outdoor planting.

USES: Good tall accent for the back of mixed beds and borders. Popular component of "all white" gardens and fragrance gardens.

NIEREMBERGIA HIPPOMANICA

COMMON NAME: Cupflower

FAMILY: Solanaceae (Nightshades)

DESCRIPTION: Native to South America. Cup-shaped, ½-inch (13mm) flowers cover low, spreading plants. Leaves are slender, indented.

HEIGHT: 6 inches (15cm).

COLOR: Purple, white.

HARDINESS: Killed by severe frost. Grows almost anywhere as a tender annual.

CULTURE: Prefers full sun, sandy or well-drained loam soil. Best grown from seed, direct-sown.

USES: Edging beds and borders; container plantings.

NIGELLA DAMASCENA

COMMON NAME: Love-in-a-mist

FAMILY: Ranunculaceae (Buttercups)

DESCRIPTION: Native to the Mediterranean region. Plants have delicate, feathery, light green leaves and cornflowerlike flowers, followed by balloonlike seed pods that are valued in dried flower arrangements.

HEIGHT: 2 feet (.6m).

COLOR: Blue, white, pink.

HARDINESS: Grows almost anywhere as a hardy annual, flowering during cool weather.

CULTURE: Prefers full sun, good drainage, sandy garden soil. Direct-sow as early in spring as possible. In mild-winter areas, sow seeds in autumn.

USES: Mixed beds and borders, old-fashioned gardens, cottage gardens, herb gardens.

NOLANA NAPIFORMIS

COMMON NAME: Nolana

FAMILY: Nolanacaea (Nolanas)

DESCRIPTION: Native to South America. Petunialike, 1-inch (2.5cm) flowers cover low, spreading plants when nights are cool.

HEIGHT: 9 inches (23cm).

COLOR: Blue.

HARDINESS: Killed by severe frost. Grows almost anywhere as a tender annual.

CULTURE: Prefers full sun, sandy or well-drained loam soil. Best grown from seed started indoors 6 weeks before outdoor planting.

USES: Edging beds and borders; container plantings.

OCIMUM BASILICUM

COMMON NAME: Basil

FAMILY: Labiatae (Mints)

DESCRIPTION: Native to North Africa. Plants are mostly grown for their decorative leaves, which may be purple or green, depending on the variety. Can be small-leaved and compact or large-leaved and tall, like coleus.

HEIGHT: 2 feet (.6m).

COLOR: Flowers are usually an inconspicuous white or pink.

HARDINESS: Killed by frost. Grows almost anywhere as a tender annual.

CULTURE: Prefers full sun and good drainage. Overwatering kills the plants. Start seed indoors 6 weeks before outdoor planting.

USES: Tall types are good for backgrounds; dwarf, compact types, for edging. The spicy leaves are popular in culinary herb gardens.

OENOTHERA SPECIOSA

COMMON NAME: Pink evening primrose

FAMILY: Onagraceae (Evening primroses)

DESCRIPTION: Native to Texas. Leaves are slender, smooth. Delicate, wispy stems are crowned with 3-inch (7.5cm), cup-shaped flowers.

HEIGHT: 12 inches (31cm).

COLOR: Pink, usually with pale pink or white centers. There is also a white form.

HARDINESS: Hardy perennial usually grown as a hardy annual. Grows almost anywhere. It can become invasive.

CULTURE: Prefers full sun, good drainage, sandy garden soil. Direct-sow. Tolerates crowding.

USES: Massing in beds and borders; also effective in wildflower meadow mixtures.

PAPAVER COMMUTATUM

COMMON NAME: Flanders poppy

FAMILY: Papaveraceae (Poppies)

DESCRIPTION: Native to Europe. Plants grow erect stems with serrated, hairy leaves and nodding flower buds, which open into a shallow cup shape to face the sun.

HEIGHT: 2 feet (.6m).

COLOR: Blood red with black spots, like a ladybird beetle.

HARDINESS: Grows almost anywhere as a hardy annual. Flowers best during cool weather.

CULTURE: Prefers full sun, well-drained loam or sandy garden soil. Direct-sow as early in spring as possible so flowering occurs before midsummer heat. Resents transplanting. In mild-winter areas, sow in autumn.

USES: Massing in beds and borders, wildflower meadows. Plants reseed freely.

PAPAVER NUDICAULE

COMMON NAME: Iceland poppy

FAMILY: Papaveraceae (Poppies)

DESCRIPTION: Native to British Columbia. Plants produce a rosette of hairy, toothed leaves that send up slender flower stems with cup-shaped flowers. Petals have the appearance of crepe paper.

HEIGHT: 2 feet (.6m).

COLOR: White, yellow, orange, pink, cream.

HARDINESS: Perennial grown mostly as a tender annual. Flowers best during cool weather.

CULTURE: Prefers full sun, good drainage. Direct-sow as early in spring as possible. In mild-winter areas, plants are best autumn-sown for extra-early spring blooms.

USES: Massing in beds and borders, naturalized plantings, cutting.

PAPAVER RHOEAS

COMMON NAME: Corn poppy

FAMILY: Papaveraceae (Poppies)

DESCRIPTION: Native to Europe. Plants are similar to Iceland poppies, but with deeper red tones and toothed leaves up the flowering stem.

HEIGHT: 2 feet (.6m).

COLOR: Red, pink, purple, white.

HARDINESS: Grows almost anywhere as a hardy annual. Flowers best during cool weather.

CULTURE: Prefers full sun, good drainage, sandy or loam garden soil. Direct-sow as early in spring as possible. Resents transplanting.

USES: Massing in beds and borders, wildflower meadows. Suitable for cutting if cut end of stem is sealed by scorching.

PAPAVER SOMNIFERUM PAEONIFLORUM

COMMON NAME: Peony poppy; opium poppy

FAMILY: Papaveraceae (Poppies)

DESCRIPTION: Native to Asia. Large, fully double, peonylike blooms are followed by large seed pods. Foliage is indented, blue-green. Late spring-flowering.

HEIGHT: 4 feet (1.2m).

COLOR: Mostly white, rose-pink, lavender.

HARDINESS: Hardy annual tolerating mild frosts. Grows best where summers are cool.

CULTURE: Needs full sun, good soil drainage. Best grown from seed, direct-sown; will not tolerate transplanting.

USES: Exquisite when mixed into perennial borders; the dried seed heads are valued by floral arrangers. Be aware that a milky sap in the seed head is a source of opium and these plants must not be cultivated as a commercial crop.

PELARGONIUM × *DOMESTICUM*

COMMON NAME: Martha Washington geranium

FAMILY: Geraniaceae (Geraniums)

DESCRIPTION: Developed from species native to South Africa. Erect plants possess ivylike leaves and a rounded cluster of 2- to 3-inch (5 to 7.5cm) flowers. Some of the individual florets resemble pansy faces.

HEIGHT: 1½ to 2 feet (.5 to .6m).

COLOR: White, rose-pink, red, purple, bicolors.

HARDINESS: Tender perennial grown mostly as a tender annual where summers are cool.

CULTURE: Prefers full sun, cool nights. Sometimes grown from cuttings. Start seeds indoors 10 weeks before outdoor planting.

USES: Beds, borders, containers, especially window boxes.

PELARGONIUM × *HORTORUM*

COMMON NAME: Zonal geranium

FAMILY: Geraniaceae (Geraniums)

DESCRIPTION: Developed from species native to South Africa. Plants grow bushy and compact, with rounded leaves and erect flower stems supporting a rounded flower cluster. Leaves are sometimes bicolored green and brown. Flowers continuously all summer.

HEIGHT: 1 to 2 feet (.3 to .6m).

COLOR: White, red, pink, orange, bicolors.

HARDINESS: Tender perennial best grown as a tender annual. Grows almost anywhere.

CULTURE: Prefers full sun, good drainage. Start seed indoors 8 weeks before outdoor planting after frost danger.

USES: Massing in beds and borders. Excellent pot plant; window boxes.

PELARGONIUM PELTATUM

COMMON NAME: Ivy geranium

FAMILY: Geraniaceae (Geraniums)

DESCRIPTION: Native to South Africa. Plants have a trailing growth habit and ivy-shaped leaves. Flowers are borne in clusters. Much more free-flowering than Martha Washington or zonal geraniums.

HEIGHT: 3 to 4 feet (.9 to 1.2m).

COLOR: White, pink, orange, red, purple.

HARDINESS: Tender perennial best treated as a tender annual.

CULTURE: Prefers full sun, good drainage, fertile soil. Mostly grown from cuttings. Start seed indoors 10 weeks before outdoor planting.

USES: Containers, hanging baskets, ground cover.

PENNISETUM SETACEUM

COMMON NAME: Fountain grass

FAMILY: Gramineae (Grasses)

DESCRIPTION: Native to Ethiopia. Plants have escaped into the wild in many warm-winter areas. A fountainlike clump of slender green leaves produces arching flower spikes resembling a bottlebrush.

HEIGHT: 4 to 5 feet (1.2 to 1.5m).

COLOR: Flowers open pink, fade to tan.

HARDINESS: Tender perennial killed by frost. Grows almost anywhere as a tender annual, though may not flower in short-season areas.

CULTURE: Prefers full sun, good drainage; tolerates poor soil, heat, drought. Start seed indoors 8 weeks before outdoor planting.

USES: Good highlight for mixed beds and borders. Effective as a temporary hedge and tall background. Good for cutting.

PENSTEMON GLOXINIOIDES

COMMON NAME: Beard-tongue

FAMILY: Scrophulariaceae (Figworts)

DESCRIPTION: Developed from species native to Mexico. Plants grow erect flower spikes with lancelike leaves and tubular flowers resembling a foxglove.

HEIGHT: 2 to 3 feet (.6 to .9m).

COLOR: White, pink, red, lavender-blue.

HARDINESS: Tender annual that flowers best in cool summers.

CULTURE: Prefers full sun, fertile loam soil, good drainage. Start seed indoors 6 to 8 weeks before outdoor planting.

USES: Beds, borders. Attractive to hummingbirds.

PERILLA FRUTESCENS

COMMON NAME: Beefsteak plant

FAMILY: Labiatae (Mints)

DESCRIPTION: Native to Southeast Asia. Bushy plants have broad, ruffled, pointed leaves with a bronze sheen. Flowers are inconspicuous.

HEIGHT: 3 to 4 feet (.9 to 1.2m).

COLOR: Purple foliage plant.

HARDINESS: Tender annual killed by frost. Seeds survive severe freezes.

CULTURE: Prefers full sun, sandy garden soil. Tolerates light shade. Drought-resistant. Direct-sow after frost danger, barely covering seeds with soil.

USES: Good background plant for annual and perennial borders.

PETUNIA × HYBRIDA GRANDIFLORA

COMMON NAME: Petunia, large-flowered

FAMILY: Solanaceae (Nightshades)

DESCRIPTION: Native to South America. Trumpet-shaped, ruffled flowers up to 6 inches (15cm) across cover low, spreading plants. Smooth, velvety, rounded leaves have a sticky texture.

HEIGHT: 12 inches (31cm).

COLOR: Red, pink, blue, yellow, white, bicolors.

HARDINESS: Killed by frost. Grows almost anywhere as a tender annual.

CULTURE: Prefers full sun, sandy or well-drained loam soil. Best grown from seed started indoors 6 to 8 weeks before outdoor planting. When plants become "leggy," they can be sheared to stimulate new flower buds.

USES: Beds, borders, window boxes, hanging baskets, other containers.

PETUNIA × *HYBRIDA MULTIFLORA*

COMMON NAME: Petunia, small-flowered

FAMILY: Solanaceae (Nightshades)

DESCRIPTION: Native to South America. Mostly smooth-petaled, trumpet-shaped blooms on low, spreading plants. Smooth, velvety, dark green leaves have a sticky texture. Flower size is usually 3 inches (7.5cm) or less.

HEIGHT: 12 inches (31cm).

COLOR: Red, pink, blue, yellow, purple, white, bicolors.

HARDINESS: Killed by frost. Grows almost anywhere as a tender annual.

CULTURE: Prefers full sun, sandy or well-drained loam soil. Best grown from seed started indoors 6 to 8 weeks before outdoor planting.

USES: Beds, borders, edging, window boxes, hanging baskets, other containers.

PETUNIA × HYBRIDA SUPERBISSIMA

COMMON NAME: Petunia California giants

FAMILY: Solanaceae (Nightshades)

DESCRIPTION: Hybrid of South American species. Largest flowers found in petunias. Ruffled petals grow up to 5 inches (13cm) across on spreading plants. Leaves are pointed, velvetlike, sticky.

HEIGHT: 12 inches (31cm).

COLOR: Purple, pink, white, bicolors.

HARDINESS: Killed by frost. Grows almost anywhere as a tender annual.

CULTURE: Prefers full sun, sandy or well-drained loam soil. Best grown from seed started indoors 6 to 8 weeks before outdoor planting.

USES: Beds, borders, containers.

PHASEOLUS COCCINEUS

COMMON NAME: Scarlet runner bean

FAMILY: Leguminosae (Peas)

DESCRIPTION: Native to South America. Plants are fast-growing vines with broad, pointed leaves arranged in trios. One-inch (2.5cm) flowers are borne in clusters, followed by edible beans.

HEIGHT: 8 to 10 feet (2.4 to 3m).

COLOR: Scarlet.

HARDINESS: Tender annual that flowers best when nights are cool.

CULTURE: Prefers full sun, sandy garden soil, cool days and nights. Direct-sow close to trellis or other support.

USES: Decorating arbors, fences, other garden structures. Dwarf forms are grown mostly in vegetable gardens.

PHLOX DRUMMONDII

COMMON NAME: Drummond phlox

FAMILY: Polemoniaceae (Phlox)

DESCRIPTION: Native to Texas. Plants are mound-shaped, grow lancelike leaves and dense clusters of star-shaped flowers, often with contrasting "eyes."

HEIGHT: 12 inches (31cm).

COLOR: Red, white, blue, pink, yellow, purple.

HARDINESS: Hardy annual that blooms best during cool weather. Will grow almost anywhere if flowering is timed for spring. Blooms 10 weeks after sowing.

CULTURE: Prefers full sun, alkaline soil. Direct-sow, or start seed indoors 8 weeks before outdoor planting.

USES: Edging beds and borders; suitable for mass bedding displays.

PIMPINELLA ANISUM

COMMON NAME: Common anise

FAMILY: Umbelliferae (Carrots)

DESCRIPTION: Native to the Mediterranean region. Plants resemble Queen-Anne's-lace, with feathery leaves and an umbel of flowers on erect stems. All parts are fragrant.

HEIGHT: 2 feet (.6m).

COLOR: White.

HARDINESS: Hardy annual that flowers best during cool weather.

CULTURE: Prefers full sun, good drainage. Direct-sow after last frost, or start seed indoors 8 weeks before outdoor planting.

USES: Mostly grown in herb gardens for its anise-flavored seeds.

PLATYCODON GRANDIFLORUS

COMMON NAME: Balloon flower

FAMILY: Campanulaceae (Bellflowers)

DESCRIPTION: Native to Japan. Plants have oval, waxy leaves on slender stalks, topped by clusters of bell-shaped flowers that develop balloonlike seed cases.

HEIGHT: 2 feet (.6m).

COLOR: Blue.

HARDINESS: Hardy perennial with one annual form: 'Blue Impression'.

CULTURE: Prefers full sun or light shade, moist soil. Start seeds early indoors 6 to 8 weeks before outdoor planting. Balloon flowers normally require two seasons to flower, but the annual form flowers the first season, will winter over, and then flower even better the next season.

USES: Mixed beds and borders. Sensational planted in light shade among moss.

POLYGONUM CAPITATUM

COMMON NAME: Trailing knotweed

FAMILY: Polygonaceae (Buckwheats)

DESCRIPTION: Native to the Himalayas. Plants form a dense, low, spreading mat of oval, pointed leaves and cloverlike, ½-inch (13mm) flowers. One plant will spread several feet and flower continuously.

HEIGHT: 4 inches (10cm).

COLOR: Pink.

HARDINESS: Killed by frost. Grows almost anywhere as a tender annual.

CULTURE: Prefers full sun, naturalizes in mild-winter areas. Direct-sow in warm soil, or start seed indoors 6 weeks before outdoor planting.

USES: Mostly used as a ground cover for hard-to-plant places such as slopes.

POLYGONUM ORIENTALE

COMMON NAME: Prince's-feather

FAMILY: Polygonaceae (Buckwheats)

DESCRIPTION: Native to Asia. Plants have naturalized on waste ground in warm-winter areas. A vigorous branching plant, possessing large, heart-shaped leaves and numerous nodding, elongated flower clusters that occur in late summer.

HEIGHT: 4 to 6 feet (1.2 to 1.8m).

COLOR: Deep rose-pink.

HARDINESS: Killed by frost. Grows almost anywhere as a tender annual. Heat-resistant.

CULTURE: Prefers full sun. Direct-sow in warm soil, or start seed indoors 6 weeks before outdoor planting.

USES: Use sparingly as a highlight in mixed beds and borders.

PORTULACA GRANDIFLORA

COMMON NAME: Rose moss

FAMILY: Portulacaceae (Purslanes)

DESCRIPTION: Native to South America. Plants have succulent trailing stems bearing plump, short leaves and cup-shaped, 2-inch (5cm) flowers. Hybrids will spread 3 feet (.9m).

HEIGHT: 6 inches (15cm).

COLOR: Red, magenta, white, yellow, orange, lavender-blue, pink.

HARDINESS: Killed by frost. Grows almost anywhere as a tender annual. Heat-resistant.

CULTURE: Prefers full sun, good drainage. Direct-sow in warm soil, or start seed 6 weeks before outdoor planting. Peak flowering lasts about 3 weeks.

USES: Massing in beds and borders.

PORTULACA OLERACEA

COMMON NAME: Purslane

FAMILY: Portulacaceae (Purslanes)

DESCRIPTION: Native to India. Plants have succulent stems with fleshy, rounded leaves and cup-shaped, ¾-inch (19mm) flowers appearing continuously all summer.

HEIGHT: 1 to 2 feet (.3 to .6m).

COLOR: Red, orange, yellow, white.

HARDINESS: Killed by frost. Grows almost anywhere as a tender annual. Heat-resistant.

CULTURE: Prefers full sun and sandy or well-drained loam soil. Tolerates high heat and humidity. Start seed indoors 8 weeks before outdoor planting.

USES: Mostly used in containers, especially hanging baskets. Makes a good temporary ground cover.

PRIMULA MALACOIDES

COMMON NAME: Fairy primrose

FAMILY: Primulaceae (Primroses)

DESCRIPTION: Developed from species native to China. Smaller-flowered than both Chinese primrose and polyanthus, the fairy primrose produces larger flower clusters and a more refined appearance. Spring-flowering.

HEIGHT: 12 inches (31cm).

COLOR: Mostly shades of pink.

HARDINESS: Tender perennial best grown as a tender annual.

CULTURE: Mostly grown as flowering pot plant for indoor decoration. Start seed indoors 10 weeks before outdoor planting. Generally unsuitable for outdoor planting, except in a Mediterranean climate because of its sensitivity to cold.

USES: Massing in beds, especially combined with daffodils in mild-climate areas. Otherwise grown as a flowering house plant.

PRIMULA OBCONICA

COMMON NAME: German primrose

FAMILY: Primulaceae (Primroses)

DESCRIPTION: Developed from species native to China. Similar in appearance to polyanthus primroses, but with broad, heart-shaped leaves and a color range that is distinctively pastel and not bicolored. Spring-flowering.

HEIGHT: 10 to 12 inches (25 to 31cm).

COLOR: Shades of pink and blue, plus white.

HARDINESS: Tender perennial best grown as a tender annual.

CULTURE: Prefers light shade, moist soil. Start seed indoors at least 10 weeks before outdoor planting. In cold-winter areas, grown mostly as an indoor flowering pot plant because of its sensitivity to frost.

USES: Useful for bedding and outdoor container plantings in mild-winter areas, but mostly grown as a flowering house plant. Excessive handling of leaves can cause mild skin irritation.

PRIMULA × POLYANTHA

COMMON NAME: Polyanthus

FAMILY: Primulaceae (Primroses)

DESCRIPTION: Hybrid of species native to Europe. Plants form rosettes of crinkled oblong leaves; produce erect, slender stems topped with clusters of 2-inch (5cm) rounded flowers in spring.

HEIGHT: 10 inches (25cm).

COLOR: Red, white, blue, yellow, pink, bicolors.

HARDINESS: Hardy perennial best grown as a hardy annual.

CULTURE: Plants prefer full sun, moist soil, cool days and nights. Seed is tiny and must be started indoors 10 weeks before outdoor planting.

USES: Edging and low bedding, especially in light shade. Also containers—especially as a flowering pot plant.

PSYLLIOSTACHYS SUWOROWII (also *LIMONIUM SUWOROWII*)

COMMON NAME: Pink pokers; Russian statice

FAMILY: Plumbaginaceae (Plumbagos)

DESCRIPTION: Native to Turkey. Grows slender leaves up to 10 inches (25cm) long with wavy margins. Flowers held erect in densely packed, pokerlike spikes, also curling like snakes. Summer-flowering.

HEIGHT: Up to 2 feet (.6m).

COLOR: Pink.

HARDINESS: Killed by frost. Grows almost anywhere as a tender annual.

CULTURE: Prefers full sun, good drainage. Direct-sow, or start indoors since seed can be slow to germinate.

USES: Mostly grown in cutting gardens for both fresh and dried floral arrangements.

PUERARIA LOBATA

COMMON NAME: Kudzu vine

FAMILY: Leguminosae (Peas)

DESCRIPTION: Native to China. Probably the world's fastest growing vine, capable of growing a foot (31cm) or more in a day. Broad, smooth, pointed leaves are arranged in trios; flowers are pealike, arranged in pointed clusters.

HEIGHT: 60 feet (18m).

COLOR: Purple.

HARDINESS: Tender perennial best grown as a tender annual. Overwinters where winters are mild.

CULTURE: Prefers full sun to flower. Direct-sow in warm soil. Requires strong support and warm, sunny summers.

USES: Decorative screen, though flowers are generally hidden by the dense leaf cover. The vine has become a wayside pest in the southern United States, where it is grown for cattle feed.

RATIBIDA COLUMNIFERA

COMMON NAME: Prairie coneflower

FAMILY: Compositae (Daisies)

DESCRIPTION: Native to midwestern United States. Resembles a black-eyed Susan, but displays an unusually long "cone" from the center of the daisylike flower. Leaves are long, slender, lancelike.

HEIGHT: 3 to 4 feet (.9 to 1.2m).

COLOR: Yellow.

HARDINESS: Grows almost anywhere as a hardy annual.

CULTURE: Prefers full sun, sandy garden soil. Direct-sow as early as possible in spring, or start seed indoors 6 weeks before outdoor planting. Will self-seed.

USES: Beds and borders; a popular component of wildflower meadow mixtures.

RESEDA ODORATA

COMMON NAME: Common mignonette

FAMILY: Resedaceae (Mignonettes)

DESCRIPTION: Native to North Africa. Bushy plants have spear-shaped leaves with a pointed cluster of small, highly fragrant flowers.

HEIGHT: 2 feet (.6m).

COLOR: Orange or rusty-red, but not conspicuous.

HARDINESS: Grows almost anywhere as a hardy annual.

CULTURE: Prefers full sun. Direct-sow in warm soil, or start indoors 6 weeks before outdoor planting.

USES: Massing as clumps in beds and borders. Also grown as a flowering pot plant.

RICINUS COMMUNIS

COMMON NAME: Castor-oil-plant

FAMILY: Euphorbiaceae (Euphorbias)

DESCRIPTION: Native to Africa. Plants grow enormous star-shaped leaves and clusters of ½-inch (13mm) spiky flowers, usually on reddish stems. Some varieties have bronze foliage. Flowers develop rounded seed pods that split to reveal bean-size seeds, which are beautifully mottled brown and white, but poisonous.

HEIGHT: 10 feet (3m).

COLOR: Red.

HARDINESS: Killed by frost. Grows almost anywhere as a tender annual.

CULTURE: Prefers full sun, hot summers, good drainage. Direct-sow into warm soil, or start indoors 4 weeks before outdoor planting.

USES: A background accent in beds and borders when used sparingly. Effective grown in large tubs.

RUDBECKIA HIRTA 'GLORIOSA DAISY'

COMMON NAME: Gloriosa daisy; black-eyed Susan

FAMILY: Compositae (Daisies)

DESCRIPTION: Developed from black-eyed Susans, a common summer-flowering North American wildflower. Plants grow daisylike flowers on slender stems with lancelike leaves.

HEIGHT: 2 to 3 feet (.6 to .9m).

COLOR: Mostly golden yellow or mahogany petals, some bicolored, surrounding a black or green "eye."

HARDINESS: Hardy perennial best grown as a hardy annual.

CULTURE: Prefers full sun, good drainage, garden soil. Direct-sow as early in spring as possible, or start seed indoors 6 to 8 weeks before outdoor planting.

USES: Massing in beds and borders.

SALPIGLOSSIS SINUATA

COMMON NAME: Painted-tongue

FAMILY: Solanaceae (Nightshades)

DESCRIPTION: Native to Chile. Plants resemble petunias but are more erect, with narrow, serrated leaves and 2-inch (5cm) flowers that are heavily veined and bicolored.

HEIGHT: 2 to 3 feet (.6 to .9m).

COLOR: Red, white, blue, yellow, orange, brown, bicolors.

HARDINESS: Tender annual. Flowers best in areas with cool summers.

CULTURE: Prefers full sun, cool days and nights. Start seed indoors 8 weeks before outdoor planting.

USES: Massing in beds and borders; popular for greenhouse culture as a winter-flowering pot plant.

SALVIA FARINACEA

COMMON NAME: Mealy-cup sage

FAMILY: Labiatae (Mints)

DESCRIPTION: Native to Texas. Erect, bushy plants have pointed, serrated, slender, blue-green leaves arranged in whorls. Square stems are topped with pointed flower clusters.

HEIGHT: 2 to 3 feet (.6 to .9m).

COLOR: Blue, white.

HARDINESS: Killed by frost. Grows almost anywhere as a tender annual.

CULTURE: Prefers full sun, good drainage; tolerates heat and drought. Start seed indoors 6 weeks before outdoor planting.

USES: Massing as a background to beds and borders. Popular for cutting.

SALVIA SPLENDENS

COMMON NAME: Scarlet sage

FAMILY: Labiatae (Mints)

DESCRIPTION: Native to Brazil. Erect plants have spear-shaped, dark green leaves and a dense flower spike formed of tubular flowers.

HEIGHT: 1 to 3 feet (.3 to .9m).

COLOR: Red, pink, white, purple.

HARDINESS: Killed by frost. Grows almost anywhere as a tender annual.

CULTURE: Prefers full sun; tolerates light shade. Start seed indoors 8 to 10 weeks before outdoor planting.

USES: Massing in beds and borders.

SALVIA VIRIDIS

COMMON NAME: Painted sage

FAMILY: Labiatae (Mints)

DESCRIPTION: Native to Europe. Erect mintlike stems and leaves have small, inconspicuous "dragons-mouth" flowers and a crown of colorful leaves that appear to be touched with paint.

HEIGHT: 1½ to 2 feet (.5 to .6m).

COLOR: Flowers are bicolored pink and white; "painted" leaves are mostly pink or blue.

HARDINESS: Killed by frost. Widely grown as a tender annual.

CULTURE: Prefers full sun. Direct-sow in warm soil, or start seed indoors 8 weeks before outdoor planting.

USES: Massing in mixed beds and borders; popular for old-fashioned cottage gardens mixed among perennials.

SANVITALIA PROCUMBENS

COMMON NAME: Creeping zinnia

FAMILY: Compositae (Daisies)

DESCRIPTION: Native to desert areas of Mexico. Plants creep along the ground, producing a dense mat of small, pointed, dark green leaves and myriad miniature (1-inch [2.5cm]) daisylike flowers all the summer season.

HEIGHT: 6 inches (15cm).

COLOR: Yellow with dark brown centers.

HARDINESS: Killed by frost. Grows almost anywhere as a tender annual.

CULTURE: Prefers full sun, good drainage. Direct-sow in warm soil.

USES: Edging beds and borders; temporary ground cover; containers—especially window boxes.

SCABIOSA ATROPURPUREA

COMMON NAME: Pincushions

FAMILY: Dipsacaceae (Teasles)

DESCRIPTION: Native to Europe. Plants grow erect stems surrounded by whorls of toothed, slender leaves and crowned with clusters of tiny flowers resembling pincushions.

HEIGHT: 2 to 3 feet (.6 to .9m).

COLOR: White, pale blue, dark purple, black, pink.

HARDINESS: Killed by frost. Grows almost anywhere as a tender annual.

CULTURE: Prefers full sun. Direct-sow in warm soil. Tolerates crowding.

USES: Massing in beds and borders. Good for cutting.

SCABIOSA STELLATA

COMMON NAME: Star flower

FAMILY: Dipsacaceae (Teasles)

DESCRIPTION: Native to the Mediterranean region. Star-shaped, 1-inch (2.5cm) flower clusters emerge from a dense clump of small, toothed leaves and quickly form a papery seed head resembling a drumstick. Continuous flowering.

HEIGHT: 18 inches (46cm).

COLOR: Pale pink, white.

HARDINESS: Killed by frost. Grows almost anywhere as a tender annual.

CULTURE: Prefers full sun. Direct-sow in warm soil.

USES: Mostly grown for cutting to create dried arrangements.

SCHIZANTHUS × WISETONENSIS

COMMON NAME: Butterfly flower

FAMILY: Solanaceae (Nightshades)

DESCRIPTION: Native to Chile. Plants grow erect, with leaves composed of many leaflets and topped with a flower spike of numerous 1-inch (2.5cm) flowers resembling miniature orchids.

HEIGHT: 2 feet (.6m).

COLOR: White, blue, pink, red, orange, yellow, bicolors, often exotically spotted.

HARDINESS: Tender annual that prefers a cool summer climate to flower well outdoors.

CULTURE: Prefers full sun or light shade and a sandy or well-drained loam soil. Intolerant of warm weather. Start seed indoors 10 weeks before outdoor planting.

USES: Though grown outdoors in mild-winter areas, plants are mostly grown under glass as a winter-flowering pot plant.

SENECIO × HYBRIDUS

COMMON NAME: Cineraria

FAMILY: Compositae (Daisies)

DESCRIPTION: Developed in England from species native to the Canary Islands. Daisylike flowers up to 3 inches (7.5cm) across cover mound-shaped plants in spring. Leaves are broad, wavy, dark green.

HEIGHT: 1 to 2 feet (.3 to .6m).

COLOR: Blue, white, red, purple, bicolors.

HARDINESS: Tender perennials grown as tender biennials and tender annuals. Killed by frost and hot weather. Mostly grown as a pot plant.

CULTURE: Prefers light shade, cool, moist, humus-rich soil. Best grown from seed started indoors 12 to 14 weeks before outdoor planting.

USES: Mostly used as flowering pot plants; also grown in beds and borders.

SILENE ARMERIA

COMMON NAME: Sweet William catchfly

FAMILY: Caryophyllaceae (Carnations)

DESCRIPTION: Native to Europe; naturalized over parts of California and Texas. Erect plants display clusters of star-shaped flowers. Leaves are lancelike, green.

HEIGHT: 18 inches (46cm).

COLOR: Mostly magenta.

HARDINESS: Grows almost anywhere as a hardy annual.

CULTURE: Prefers full sun, good drainage, sandy garden soil. Direct-sow.

USES: Mixed borders, rock gardens, meadow wildflower gardens.

SILYBUM MARIANUM

COMMON NAME: St. Mary's thistle

FAMILY: Compositae (Daisies)

DESCRIPTION: Native to the Mediterranean region. Plants are grown mostly for their attractive, mottled, white and blue-green spiny leaves, which create a silvery effect. The flowers, 2½ inches (6.5cm) across, are typical of thistles and are usually not produced until the second season.

HEIGHT: 3 to 4 feet (.9 to 1.2m).

COLOR: Flowers are purple, nodding, not ornamental.

HARDINESS: Grows almost anywhere as a hardy annual.

CULTURE: Prefers full sun, good drainage, sandy garden soil. Direct-sow.

USES: Mixed borders, herb gardens. Popular in all-white gardens.

SOLANUM MELONGENA

COMMON NAME: Ornamental eggplant

FAMILY: Solanaceae (Nightshades)

DESCRIPTION: Native to South America. Mostly egg-shaped fruits follow star-shaped white or pink flowers. Leaves are coarse, prickly, pointed.

HEIGHT: 2 to 3 feet (.6 to .9m).

COLOR: Fruits are white, yellow, red, purple.

HARDINESS: Killed by frost. Grows almost anywhere as a tender annual.

CULTURE: Prefers full sun, sandy or well-drained loam soil. Best grown from seed started indoors 6 to 8 weeks before outdoor planting.

USES: Beds, borders, containers.

TAGETES ERECTA

COMMON NAME: American marigold; African marigold

FAMILY: Compositae (Daisies)

DESCRIPTION: Native to Mexico. Mostly globular flowers up to 5 inches (13cm) across bloom nonstop all summer on bushy plants. Spicy, serrated, dark green leaves are a natural insect repellent.

HEIGHT: 2 to 3 feet (.6 to .9m).

COLOR: White, yellow, gold, orange.

HARDINESS: Killed by frost. Grows almost anywhere as a tender annual.

CULTURE: Prefers full sun, sandy or well-drained loam soil with low fertility; tolerates high heat. Direct-sow, or start seed indoors 6 weeks before outdoor planting.

USES: Beds, borders, containers, cutting.

TAGETES PATULA

COMMON NAME: French marigold

FAMILY: Compositae (Daisies)

DESCRIPTION: Native to Mexico. Mostly rounded, double flowers 1 to 2 inches (2.5 to 5cm) across bloom continuously on low, mounded plants. Indented dark green leaves emit a spicy odor when bruised.

HEIGHT: 1 to 2 feet (.3 to .6m).

COLOR: Rusty red, yellow, orange, bicolors.

HARDINESS: Killed by severe frost. Grows almost anywhere as a tender annual.

CULTURE: Prefers full sun, sandy or well-drained loam soil. Best grown from seed, direct-sown or started indoors 4 to 6 weeks before outdoor planting.

USES: Beds, borders, edging, cutting.

TAGETES TENUIFOLIA (also **TAGETES SIGNATA**)

COMMON NAME: Signet marigold

FAMILY: Compositae (Daisies)

DESCRIPTION: Native to Mexico. Plants grow into neat mounds. Leaves, made up of numerous narrow, pointed leaflets, emit a spicy odor repellent to insects. Flowers are mostly single, five-petaled, continuous all summer.

HEIGHT: 12 to 18 inches (31 to 46cm).

COLOR: Mostly yellow, gold, rusty red, bicolors.

HARDINESS: Killed by severe frost. Grows almost anywhere as a tender annual.

CULTURE: Prefers full sun, good drainage. Direct-sow in warm soil, or start seed 6 weeks before outdoor planting.

USES: Edging beds and borders; also rock gardens, containers.

163

TAGETES TRIPLOID HYBRIDS

COMMON NAME: Mule marigolds; Afro-French marigolds

FAMILY: Compositae (Daisies)

DESCRIPTION: Developed from species native to Mexico. A cross between *Tagetes erecta* and *Tagetes patula*, plants are similar to French marigolds but are more vigorous, larger-flowered, and more free-flowering. Plants are mound-shaped; flowers are sterile, bloom early, and continue nonstop until autumn frost.

HEIGHT: 1 to 2 feet (.3 to .6m).

COLOR: Mostly yellow, gold, rusty red, bicolors.

HARDINESS: Killed by frost. Grows almost anywhere as a tender annual.

CULTURE: Prefers full sun. Seed germination can be substandard, so start seed indoors 6 weeks before outdoor planting.

USES: Massing in beds and borders, edging paths, container plantings.

THUNBERGIA ALATA

COMMON NAME: Black-eyed Susan vine

FAMILY: Acanthaceae (Acanthus)

DESCRIPTION: Native to Africa. Plants have fast growing, twining stems with heart-shaped leaves and 1½-inch (4cm), five-petaled flowers with black throats.

HEIGHT: 10 feet (3m).

COLOR: Yellow, white.

HARDINESS: Killed by frost. Grows almost anywhere as a tender annual. Perennial in frost-free areas.

CULTURE: Prefers full sun or light shade. Start seed indoors 8 weeks before outdoor planting. Provide strong supports.

USES: Decorating trellises, arbors, fences; also good for hanging baskets, as a winter-flowering pot plant.

TITHONIA ROTUNDIFOLIA

COMMON NAME: Mexican sunflower

FAMILY: Compositae (Daisies)

DESCRIPTION: Native to Mexico. Daisylike flowers up to 4 inches (10cm) across flower from midsummer atop long, strong stems, forming bushy plants. Leaves are heart-shaped, dark green.

HEIGHT: 4 to 6 feet (1.2 to 1.8m).

COLOR: Orange.

HARDINESS: Killed by frost. Grows almost anywhere as a tender annual.

CULTURE: Prefers full sun, sandy or well-drained loam soil. Best grown from seed, direct-sown.

USES: Tall backgrounds for beds and borders.

TORENIA FOURNIERI

COMMON NAME: Wishbone flower

FAMILY: Scrophulariaceae (Figworts)

DESCRIPTION: Native to Vietnam. Pansylike, ½-inch (13mm) flowers have a curious wishbone arrangement inside the throat. Serrated, pointed, dark green leaves create mounded plants.

HEIGHT: 12 inches (31cm).

COLOR: Blue, white, pink.

HARDINESS: Killed by frost. Grows almost anywhere as a tender annual.

CULTURE: Prefers light shade, cool, moist, humus-rich soil. Best grown from seed started indoors 8 to 10 weeks before outdoor planting.

USES: Shady beds and borders, edging, containers.

TRACHELIUM CAERULEUM

COMMON NAME: Throatwort

FAMILY: Campanulaceae (Bellflowers)

DESCRIPTION: Native to southern Europe. Plants resemble ageratum; produce 4- to 5-inch (10 to 13cm) umbels of closely packed, star-shaped flowers on strong stems with lancelike leaves.

HEIGHT: 2 to 3 feet (.6 to .9m).

COLOR: Purple.

HARDINESS: Killed by frost. Grows almost anywhere as a tender annual. Perennial in frost-free areas.

CULTURE: Prefers full sun. Direct-sow in warm soil, or start seed indoors 8 weeks before outdoor planting.

USES: Massing in beds and borders. Excellent cut flower.

TRACHYMENE COERULEA

COMMON NAME: Blue lace flower

FAMILY: Umbelliferae (Carrots)

DESCRIPTION: Native to Australia. Plants resemble Queen-Anne's-lace, with tiny flowers in flat umbels up to 3½ inches (9cm) across. Leaves are narrow, toothed.

HEIGHT: 2 feet (.6m).

COLOR: Pale blue.

HARDINESS: Hardy annual that requires cool conditions to flower.

CULTURE: Prefers full sun. Direct-sow in garden soil as early in spring as possible.

USES: Massing in beds and borders. Suitable for cutting.

TRIFOLIUM INCARNATUM

COMMON NAME: Crimson clover

FAMILY: Leguminosae (Peas)

DESCRIPTION: Native to Europe. Grows erect, cloverlike plants with oval leaflets arranged in trios. Conspicuous 2½-inch (6.5cm), candlelike flower clusters are produced in profusion in early summer.

HEIGHT: Up to 3 feet (.9m).

COLOR: Crimson.

HARDINESS: Tolerates freezing. Grows almost anywhere as a hardy annual.

CULTURE: Prefers full sun; tolerates poor soil. Direct-sow. Tolerates crowding.

USES: Massing as a ground cover; also used as an ornamental cover crop in vegetable gardens to fix nitrogen into the soil.

TRITICUM AESTIVUM

COMMON NAME: Ornamental wheat

FAMILY: Gramineae (Grasses)

DESCRIPTION: Native to western Asia. Plants grow grasslike leaves and erect stems topped by a flower spike, which develops a cluster of fat grains evenly spaced, with "whiskers."

HEIGHT: 2 to 3 feet (.6 to .9m).

COLOR: Brown when mature.

HARDINESS: Hardy annual best planted in autumn in mild-winter climates to mature over winter; sow in spring elsewhere.

CULTURE: Prefers full sun. Direct-sow in fertile loam soil with good drainage. Tolerates crowding.

USES: Mostly used for cutting and dried arrangements.

TROPAEOLUM MAJUS

COMMON NAME: Nasturtium

FAMILY: Tropaeolaceae (Nasturtiums)

DESCRIPTION: Native to South America. Mostly four-petaled, 3-inch (7.5cm) flowers bloom continuously on mounded or vining plants, depending on variety. Rounded, bright green leaves resemble a parasol.

HEIGHT: 2 to 6 feet (.6 to 1.8m).

COLOR: Red, orange, yellow, pink, white, cream, mahogany.

HARDINESS: Tender annual killed by frost. Grows almost anywhere as an annual.

CULTURE: Prefers full sun, cool, moist soil with low fertility. Best grown from seed, direct-sown. Also propagated from cuttings. Flowers when nights are cool.

USES: Beds, borders, containers, cutting.

TROPAEOLUM PEREGRINUM

COMMON NAME: Canary-bird flower

FAMILY: Tropaeolaceae (Nasturtiums)

DESCRIPTION: Native to South America. Fast-growing vines of palmate leaves possess lovely 1-inch (2.5cm) flowers that resemble a bird in flight.

HEIGHT: 8 feet (2.4m).

COLOR: Yellow with red spots.

HARDINESS: Killed by frost. Grows almost anywhere as a tender annual.

CULTURE: Prefers full sun. Direct-sow in warm soil, or start indoors 6 weeks before outdoor planting.

USES: Decorating trellises, arbors, fences.

URSINIA ANTHEMOIDES

COMMON NAME: African daisy, dill-leaf daisy.

FAMILY: Compositae (Daisies)

DESCRIPTION: Native to South Africa. Plants grow fernlike leaves and daisylike flowers on erect stems.

HEIGHT: 18 inches (46cm).

COLOR: Yellow and red bicolored.

HARDINESS: Moderately hardy, but killed by severe frost. Demands cool conditions.

CULTURE: Prefers full sun. In mild-winter areas, direct-sow in autumn for early spring flowering.

USES: Massing in beds and borders.

VENIDIUM FASTUOSUM

COMMON NAME: Cape daisy

FAMILY: Compositae (Daisies)

DESCRIPTION: Native to South Africa. Plants have indented leaves like a chrysanthemum and 4-inch (10cm), daisylike flowers.

HEIGHT: 18 inches (46cm).

COLOR: Yellow or white, with a dark chocolate-colored zone around a yellow-rimmed black eye.

HARDINESS: Moderately hardy annual killed by severe frost. Grows best where summers are cool.

CULTURE: Prefers full sun, good drainage. Direct-sow in warm soil. In mild-winter areas, sow in autumn for extra-early spring flowers.

USES: Massing in beds and borders. Excellent cut flower.

VERBENA × *HYBRIDA*

COMMON NAME: Garden verbena

FAMILY: Verbenaceae (Verbenas)

DESCRIPTION: Native to South America. Plants have pointed, serrated leaves and small primroselike flowers that form a round, flat flower head.

HEIGHT: 12 inches (31cm).

COLOR: Red, white, blue, pink, beige—many with a contrasting "eye."

HARDINESS: Killed by frost. Grows almost anywhere as a tender annual.

CULTURE: Prefers full sun or light shade. Soil should be sandy or well-drained loam. Start seed indoors 8 weeks before outdoor planting since germination is generally substandard and direct seeding is unreliable.

USES: Massing in beds and borders. Some trailing kinds are suitable for hanging baskets and ground cover.

VERBENA PERUVIANA

COMMON NAME: Creeping verbena

FAMILY: Verbenaceae (Verbenas)

DESCRIPTION: Native to Argentina and Brazil. Plants have narrow, toothed leaves and masses of 1½-inch (4cm) flower clusters, with individual florets resembling a small primrose.

HEIGHT: 6 inches (15cm).

COLOR: Bright red.

HARDINESS: Killed by frost. Grows almost anywhere as a tender annual.

CULTURE: Prefers full sun or light shade. Soil should be sandy or well-drained loam. Start seed indoors 8 weeks before outdoor planting.

USES: Bed and border edging; hanging baskets; temporary ground cover.

VIOLA CORNUTA

COMMON NAME: Horned viola

FAMILY: Violaceae (Violets)

DESCRIPTION: Native to the mountains of southern Europe. Plants form a rosette of scalloped, oval leaves and 1½-inch (4cm) flowers with flat faces.

HEIGHT: 6 inches (15cm).

COLOR: Red, white, blue, purple, yellow. White is sometimes "whiskered" with black streaks.

HARDINESS: Hardy annual that blooms best during cool weather.

CULTURE: Prefers full sun or light shade, cool nights, and a humus-rich loam soil. Start seed indoors 10 weeks before outdoor planting; or start seed in autumn, holding in a cold frame for planting out in bloom.

USES: Massing in beds and borders; edging; containers.

VIOLA TRICOLOR

COMMON NAME: Johnny-jump-up

FAMILY: Violaceae (Violets)

DESCRIPTION: Native to Europe. Plants form clumps of oval leaves and masses of tricolored, five-petaled, ½-inch (13mm) flowers resembling tiny pansies.

HEIGHT: 12 inches (31cm).

COLOR: Top two petals are purple; two side petals are white; lower petal is yellow.

HARDINESS: Hardy perennial grown as a hardy annual.

CULTURE: Prefers sun or light shade, cool conditions and a humus-rich loam soil. Start seed indoors 10 weeks before outdoor planting. Can be direct-sown in late summer for extra-early spring flowering. Self-sows freely.

USES: Massing in beds and borders.

VIOLA × WITTROCKIANA

COMMON NAME: Pansy

FAMILY: Violaceae (Violets)

DESCRIPTION: Developed from species native to Europe. Plants form rosettes of serrated, lancelike leaves and erect stems with flat five-petaled flowers up to 5 inches (13cm) across.

HEIGHT: 12 inches (31cm).

COLOR: White, red, blue, yellow, orange, purple—some clear colors, others with conspicuous black markings.

HARDINESS: Hardy perennial best grown as a hardy annual. Grows almost anywhere during cool weather.

CULTURE: Grows in sun or light shade and a humus-rich loam soil. Start seed indoors 10 weeks before outdoor planting. Mostly spring-flowering, though some varieties are everblooming and will continue to bloom even into winter months.

USES: Beds, borders, containers, edging.

ZEA MAYS

COMMON NAME: Indian corn

FAMILY: Gramineae (Grasses)

DESCRIPTION: Developed from now-extinct species native to Mexico. Plants grow tall stalks with arching, straplike green or variegated white-and-green leaves. Tassellike male flowers are at top of the plant, and silky threadlike female flowers are at leaf internodes. Following pollination, decorative seed clusters called cobs are formed.

HEIGHT: 10 feet (3m).

COLOR: When grown for the decorative cobs, colors can be yellow, white, red, black, or blue—often with several colors in the same cob.

HARDINESS: Killed by frost. Grows almost anywhere as a tender annual.

CULTURE: Prefers full sun. Direct-sow in fertile loam soil.

USES: Dried cobs mostly used for Thanksgiving decoration.

XERANTHEMUM ANNUUM

COMMON NAME: Immortelle

FAMILY: Compositae (Daisies)

DESCRIPTION: Native to the Mediterranean region. Slender stems bear daisylike flowers with pointed, papery petals. Leaves are slender, toothed.

HEIGHT: 2 to 3 feet (.6 to .9m).

COLOR: White, pink, purple, red with yellow "eyes."

HARDINESS: Hardy annual that blooms best during cool weather.

CULTURE: Prefers full sun, sandy soil. Direct-sow in early spring.

USES: Massing in mixed beds and borders. Excellent for cutting and dried arrangements.

ZINNIA ANGUSTIFOLIA

COMMON NAME: Classic zinnia

FAMILY: Compositae (Daisies)

DESCRIPTION: Native to Mexico. Small daisylike, 1-inch (2.5cm) flowers are borne in great profusion on low, spreading, mounded plants with slender, dark green leaves.

HEIGHT: 8 to 12 inches (20 to 31cm).

COLOR: Orange.

HARDINESS: Killed by frost. Grows almost anywhere as a tender annual.

CULTURE: Prefers full sun and sandy or loam soil that drains well. Best grown from seed, direct-sown.

USES: Good temporary ground cover planted in a mass. Also suitable for edging beds and borders and container plantings.

ZINNIA ELEGANS 'CACTUS-FLOWERED'

COMMON NAME: Cactus-flowered zinnia

FAMILY: Compositae (Daisies)

DESCRIPTION: Native to Mexico. Branching plants possess erect flower stems and spear-shaped, dark green leaves. Large 5-inch (13cm) flowers have quilled petals during summer.

HEIGHT: Up to 3½ feet (1.1m).

COLOR: White, yellow, orange, red, pink, purple.

HARDINESS: Killed by frost. Grows almost anywhere as an annual, especially where summers are warm and sunny.

CULTURE: Prefers full sun, well-drained sandy or loam soil. Direct-sow, thinning to 12 inches (31cm) apart (plants will wilt from careless transplanting).

USES: Massing in beds and borders. Good for cutting.

ZINNIA ELEGANS 'DAHLIA-FLOWERED'

COMMON NAME: Dahlia-flowered zinnia

FAMILY: Compositae (Daisies)

DESCRIPTION: Native to Mexico. Flowers resemble dahlias, with rounded petal tips; other flower forms are available. Blooms measure up to 5 inches (13cm) across, continuing from mid-summer to autumn frost. Plants make strong upright growth, have dark green lancelike leaves.

HEIGHT: 1 to 3 feet (.3 to .9m).

COLOR: Yellow, orange, white, green, red, pink, purple, bicolors.

HARDINESS: Killed by frost. Grows almost anywhere as a tender annual, especially where summers are warm and sunny.

CULTURE: Prefers full sun, well-drained loam soil. Best grown from seed, direct-sown.

USES: Beds, borders, cutting. Dwarf types suitable for containers.

ZINNIA HAAGEANA

COMMON NAME: Mexican zinnia

FAMILY: Compositae (Daisies)

DESCRIPTION: Native to Mexico. Grows bushy plants with spear-shaped, dark green leaves and masses of 2-inch (5cm), daisylike flowers with pointed petals. Summer-flowering.

HEIGHT: Up to 2 feet (.6m).

COLOR: Mostly yellow and red bicolors.

HARDINESS: Killed by frost. Grows almost anywhere as an annual, especially where summers are warm and sunny.

CULTURE: Prefers full sun, well-drained sandy or loam soil. Direct-sow, thinning to 12 inches (31cm) apart.

USES: Massing in mixed beds and borders. Good for cutting and containers.

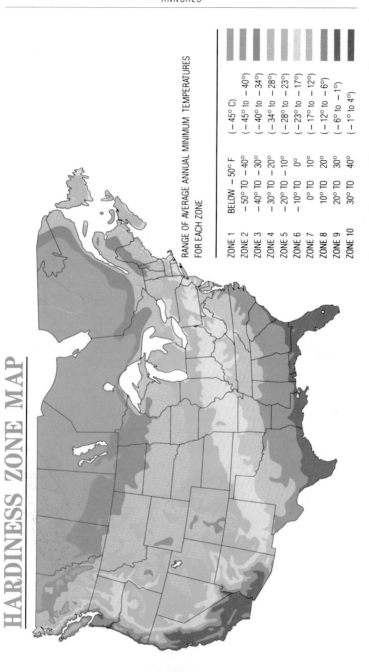

HARDINESS ZONE MAP

RANGE OF AVERAGE ANNUAL MINIMUM TEMPERATURES
FOR EACH ZONE

ZONE 1	BELOW −50° F	(−45° C)
ZONE 2	−50° TO −40°	(−45° to −40°)
ZONE 3	−40° TO −30°	(−40° to −34°)
ZONE 4	−30° TO −20°	(−34° to −28°)
ZONE 5	−20° TO −10°	(−28° to −23°)
ZONE 6	−10° TO 0°	(−23° to −17°)
ZONE 7	0° TO 10°	(−17° to −12°)
ZONE 8	10° TO 20°	(−12° to −6°)
ZONE 9	20° TO 30°	(−6° to −1°)
ZONE 10	30° TO 40°	(−1° to 4°)

INDEX

Rhodanthe. See *Helipterum roseum.*
Ricinus communis, 150
Rocket larkspur. See *Consolida ambigua.*
Rose mallow. See *Hibiscus moscheutos;*
 Lavatera trimestris.
Rose moss. See *Portulaca grandiflora.*
Rose-of-heaven. See *Lynchis coeli-rosa.*
Rudbeckia hirta 'Gloriosa Daisy', 151
Runner bean. See *Phaseolus coccineus.*
Russian statice. See *Psylliostachys*
 suworowii.

S

Sage. See *Lantana camara* hybrids; *Salvia*
 farinacea; Salvia splendens; Salvia viridis.
St. Mary's thistle. See *Silybum marianum.*
Salpiglossis sinuata, 152
Salvia farinacea, 152
Salvia splendens, 153
Salvia viridis, 154
Sanvitalia procumbens, 155
Satin flower. See *Clarkia amoena.*
Scabiosa atropurpurea, 156
Scabiosa stellata, 157
Scarlet flax. See *Limum grandiflorum.*
Scarlet runner bean. See *Phaseolus*
 coccineus.
Scarlet sage. See *Salvia splendens.*
Schizanthus x *wisetonensis,* 157
Scrambled eggs. See *Limnanthes douglasii.*
Senecio x *hybridus,* 158
Shasta daisy. See *Chrysanthemum*
 maximum.
Shoo-fly plant. See *Nicandra physalodes.*
Siberian wallflower. See *Erysimum*
 hieraciifolium.
Signet marigold. See *Tagetes tenuifolia.*
Silene armeria, 159
Silene coeli-rosa, 107
Silybum marianum, 160
Small-flowered petunia. See *Petunia* x *hybrida*
 multiflora.

Snapdragon. See *Antirrhinum majus.*
Snow-on-the-mountain. See *Euphorbia*
 marginata.
Solanum melongena, 161
Spider flower. See *Cleome hasslerana.*
Star flower. See *Scabiosa stellata.*
Statice. See *Limonium sinuatum;*
 Psylliostachys suworowii.

Stock. See *Malcolmia maritima; Matthiola*
 incana; Matthiola longipetala bicornis.
Strawberry. See *Fragaria vesca.*
Strawflower. See *Helichrysum bracteatum.*
Summer forget-me-not. See *Anchusa*
 capensis.
Sunflower. See *Helianthus annuus;*
 Helianthus annuus 'Teddy Bear';
 Helianthus intermedius; Tithonia
 rotundifolia.
Swamp mallow. See *Hibiscus moscheutos.*
Swan River daisy. See *Brachycome*
 iberidifolia.
Sweet alyssum. See *Lobularia maritima.*
Sweet pea. See *Lathyrus odoratus.*
Sweet-sultan. See *Centaurea moschata.*
Sweet William. See *Dianthus barbatus.*
Sweet William catchfly. See *Silene armeria.*

T

Tagetes erecta, 162
Tagetes patula, 162
Tagetes signata, 163
Tagetes tenuifolia, 163
Tagetes triploid hybrids, 164
Tahoka daisy. See *Machaeranthera*
 tanacetifolia.
Tassel flower. See *Emilia javanica.*
Texas bluebonnet. See *Lupinus texensis.*
Thistle. See *Silybum marianum.*
Thorn apple. See *Datura metel.*
Throatwort. See *Trachelium caeruleum.*
Thunbergia alata, 165